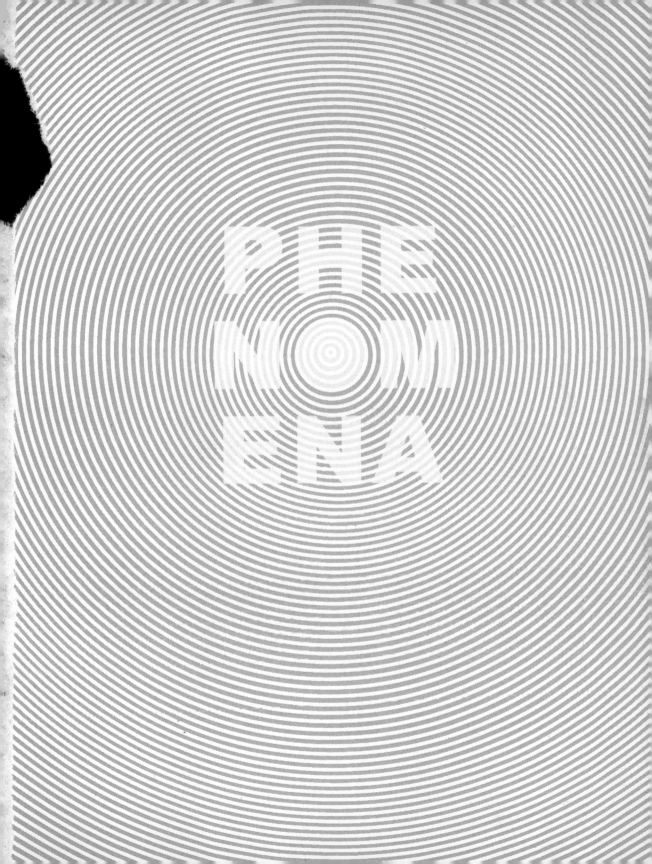

PHENOMENA

SECRETS OF THE SENSES

by Donna M. Jackson

LITTLE, BROWN AND COMPANY

Books for Young Readers

New York   Boston

In memory of Charlotte Foltz Jones, a dear friend and mentor

Little, Brown Books for Young Readers

Hachette Book Group USA
237 Park Avenue, New York, NY 10017
Visit our Web site at www.lb-kids.com

First U.S. Edition: September 2008

ISBN 978-0-316-16649-2

10 9 8 7 6 5 4 3 2 1

RRD-C

Designed by Tracy Shaw

Printed in the United States of America

Little, Brown Books for Young Readers is a division of Hachette Book Group USA, Inc.
The Little, Brown logo is a trademark of Hachette Book Group USA, Inc.

ACKNOWLEDGMENTS

Many generous people worldwide have shared their experiences, expertise, and images for this book. My heartfelt thanks to the following for thoughtfully taking time to tell their stories and conveying their knowledge in words and pictures: Dr. Jonathan Cole, Ian Waterman, Dr. A. James Hudspeth, Dr. Vilayanur Ramachandran, Carol Crane, Sean Day, Dr. Richard Cytowic, Edward Hubbard, Julia Simner, Esref Armagan, Joan Eroncel, John M. Kennedy, Dr. Alvaro Pascual-Leone, Pat Fletcher, Peter Meijer, Linda Muszynski, Tom Whittaker, Cheryl Schiltz, Yuri Danilov, Dr. Anil Raj, Karl Sigman, Hollis Long, Josh Tenenbaum, Sam Gosling, Thomas Gilovich, David G. Myers, Richard Wiseman, Ronald Rensink, Annette Martin, Athena Drewes, John Palmer, Rita Dwyer, Robert Van de Castle, Rosalind Cartwright, Caitlin O'Connell-Rodwell, Bill Barklow, Michelle Heupel, John Caprio, Debbie Marvit-McGlothin, Nicholas Broffman, Kathy Hill, Edith Resnick, Jep Enck, Gail Bishop, Lydia Kibiuk, Andy Manis, Matthew Wilson, Richard Masland, Rebecca Harkin, Tracey Somers, Anthony Freeman, David Simpson, Slawomir Grünberg, Zafer Kizilkaya, Dianne Patterson, Linda Briscoe, Cathy Strange, Eric Chudler, Shelley and Lauren Frihauf, Elif Ozdemir, Barbara Schweizer, David E. Simpson, Zafer Kizikaya, Cindy VanHorn, Brandi Dean, Yvette Reyes, Sona Walters and Ashley Morton.

A special thanks to Megan Tingley and Nancy Conescu at Little, Brown for sensing the book's potential; Tracy Shaw for her "phenomenal" design; Lauren Hodge for her editorial assistance; and to Charlie Jackson, whose love and support echo through the pages.

As we acquire more knowledge,
things do not become more comprehensible,
but more mysterious.

— Albert Schweitzer, philosopher, physician, humanitarian

CONTENTS

SENSING THE WORLD

an Waterman of England seldom thought twice about his senses. Like most people, he took them for granted. That is, until age nineteen, when a flu-like viral infection sapped his sensations from below the neck. "I just fell in a crumpled heap," he says. "Like a puppet with no strings."

A few days later, Ian was hospitalized. But instead of getting better, his condition deteriorated. "My first night in the hospital seemed to be the ebbing away of all that was normal in relationship to movement," he says. "I'd become sort of disembodied. . . . You know, I was a head without a body. I had no control over what was normally under my jurisdiction." Doctors didn't seem to have any answers either. That really scared him. After weeks of physical therapy, he says, "It became fairly clear nothing was happening."

Turns out, Ian suffered from a rare illness that stole his body's unconscious awareness of itself and its movable parts. Ian was "floppy" and lived in a "limbless limbo," says neurophysiologist Dr. Jonathan Cole. "Not only couldn't he feel anything to touch, he had no idea where the various bits of his body were without looking at them." Ian could move, he just couldn't instinctively control or coordinate those movements because his brain wasn't receiving sensory feedback to help him monitor his actions. Communication between his brain and body had broken down.

Through the years and against all odds, Ian trained himself to carefully choreograph each movement he made using vision as his guide. "Once you realize the damage is done, you get on with it," he says. By looking at his limbs and concentrating on making his body move, Ian eventually learned to sit up, stand, and drive a car. "I became the ultimate control freak," he says. Of the ten known people in the world with this condition, Ian's believed to be the only one who has taught himself to walk.

At age nineteen, Ian Waterman lost his sense of proprioception—the body's unconscious awareness of itself and its movable parts.

Photo courtesy of Ian Waterman

INNER COMPASSES

Our senses help us navigate the world. Working in concert, they feed important information to the brain about what's happening to, and around, our bodies. The simplest of acts — such as recognizing and waving hello to a friend — require hundreds of millions of sensory nerve cells, called neurons, to communicate with the brain so that we can instantly read and react to situations.

While the primary five senses — vision, hearing, touch, taste, and smell — are most obvious, at least twenty-one have been identified. We have a sense of hunger, thirst, balance, and fatigue. We sense pain, temperature, and muscle tension. We even have senses that detect pressure in our gut and bladder, as well as those that adjust our heartbeat and measure the levels of oxygen and carbon dioxide in our blood. These senses keep the body running smoothly.

Our senses help us experience the world and often bring us pleasure.

© Blend Images

Our senses help us consciously create and experience the world. They bring us pleasure: tender touches, sparkling skies, and the rhythmic rhapsodies of music. They alert us to dangers: screeching tires, a flash of lightning, and the pungent odor of natural gas. Our senses also enable us to distinguish sweet from sour, hot from cold, and light from dark.

Even before we're born, sensations offer us a window to the world. Our sense of touch begins developing at about eight weeks after conception. Soon we're sucking our thumbs and exploring our faces with our fingers. By about eighteen weeks, we hear our mother's breathing and the *tha-thump, tha-thump* of her heartbeat. This calming cadence appears in other areas of our lives, notes Jillyn Smith in her book *Senses and Sensibilities.* "It has been suggested that children begin to speak in double syllables — da-da, ma-ma — in imitation of the paired heartbeat sounds, and that a child instinctively clings to the left side, the heartbeat side, of the mother's breast."

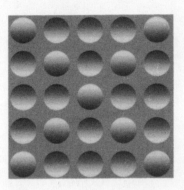

See an X made of circles that pop out? It's an optical illusion. Our brains sense that light shines from above, so the circles that are shaded lighter on top seem to stand out, while those that are shaded darker on top recede. Turn the page upside down and watch what happens.

Mark R. Holmes,
© National Geographic Society

Yet while we all live in the same physical world, each of us experiences it uniquely, says psychologist and professor Francis B. Colavita of the University of Pittsburgh. Not only do our senses respond to different elements in the environment, our brains assign different meanings to the same sensations. "A perception is a sensation plus its unique meaning for an individual," explains Colavita. "Two people may be exposed to the same sensory (information), but their differing personalities, cultural backgrounds, expectations, motivational and emotional states, family histories, and life experiences will determine how similar or different their perceptions of that sensory [information] will be." A person who's recently been in a car accident, for example, is more apt to flinch when an ambulance races by than someone who hasn't suffered the same trauma.

Individually, we also experience different "realities" throughout our lifetimes as we continually grow and develop. Our sensory systems age and evolve along with us, says Colavita, so what tasted great at seven may not be so appetizing at seventy.

DECIPHERING THE BIG PICTURE

One major mystery of neuroscience is how the brain, which contains about 100 billion nerve cells, processes all the sensory signals it receives in fragments and unifies them as a whole into our overall perceptions. Scientists refer to this as "the binding problem."

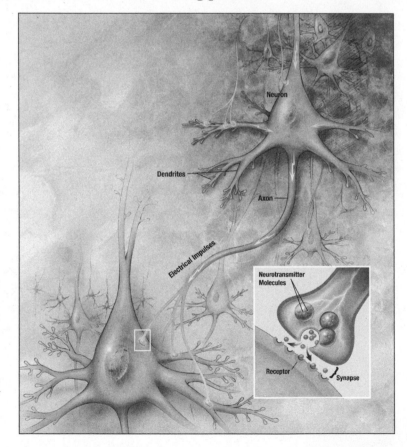

Our brains contain billions of nerve cells, or neurons, that constantly communicate with each other via electrical signals. Different neurons hold different jobs. Some help coordinate muscle movements, while others take in messages from our senses.

Courtesy of the Alzheimer's Disease Education and Referral (ADEAR) Center

Visual images, for example, may be parallel-processed in twenty-five or more regions of the brain, each with a specialized job such as color identification, depth perception, and motion detection. "Yet somehow the brain pulls it back together," says Dr. A. James Hudspeth, a researcher for the Howard Hughes Medical Institute and head of the Laboratory of Sensory Neuroscience at the Rockefeller University in New York. "In addition to seeing the particular color of your skin and hair and the particular outlines of your face and how far away you are, and whether or not you're moving and so on, I'm able to see all the pieces together and identify you."

Always at work, our brains make educated guesses that fill in the blanks where needed. That's why you see triangles in the above image.

Mark R. Holmes,
© National Geographic Society

And that's just one sense. Factor in messages flooding in from what you're hearing, smelling, and touching — along with inputs from your memories, previous experiences, and the context of the situation — and the brain's making multifaceted connections and shaping perceptions with astonishing speed and precision.

"We still don't know how this operates," says Dr. Hudspeth. "But it is known that beyond the simpler parts of the cerebral cortex, there are a number of association areas that are sensitive to more than one sense at the same time. So they may be excited by sound or by a visual stimulus or by touch simultaneously." This leads to the theory

"One of our most striking senses is equilibrium or balance," says Dr. A. James Hudspeth, a researcher for the Howard Hughes Medical Institute. "Our capacity to stand upright, for example, depends critically on feedback from the inner ear—the vestibular labyrinth—which constantly measures our body's position and whether it's beginning to fall one way or another."

© AP Wide World Photos

that the association cortex, which is involved in higher processing of information, is responsible somehow for pulling together our perceptions.

Emotions also influence our perceptions of the world. Seeing a close friend or relative generally elicits a myriad of feelings associated with that person. After we've identified someone visually, for example, the message moves to the amygdala, an area of the brain that helps us determine a person's emotional significance.

People with Capras syndrome, however, lose this emotional connection. This rare neurological condition — often the result of a severe head injury — appears to damage the neural pathways between the visual and emotional centers of the brain, explains Dr. Vilayanur Ramachandran, director of the Center for Brain and Cognition at the University of California, San Diego. As a result, those afflicted believe the people closest to them are imposters.

One man injured in a car accident thought his mother was an imposter. "Doctor, this woman looks exactly like my mother but she isn't," he insisted. Since the man didn't feel appropriate emotions when he saw his mother, he decided she must be someone pretending to be her. When the man's mother telephoned him an hour later, however, he immediately recognized her and her voice. Apparently, the auditory path to the emotional center had remained intact.

Conditions such as Capras syndrome offer scientists an opportunity to learn more about the workings of the brain. They also offer compelling examples of how our perceptions are not only shaped by the sensory information we receive, but by *how* the information is processed and interpreted in the brain.

MIND BOGGLERS

Our senses hold many secrets, and questions abound about the extent of their capabilities. Many unexplained phenomena, for instance, have roots in our sensations and the way the brain understands them through our perceptions.

Some people report near-death experiences, such as feeling a deep sense of peace or seeing bright lights at the end of a dark tunnel. Others say they've seen ghosts haunting houses and castles or have witnessed unidentified flying objects (UFOs) suspended in the skies. More common are those who describe having a sense of being stared at from afar or experiencing déjà vu — the feeling that a new situation has happened before. Incidents like these are said to be extrasensory, or beyond our normal senses. Often, they're referred to as involving a "sixth sense." Gut instincts that guide many of our life decisions, such as choosing friends, also fall into this category, as do nightly dreams that seemingly predict the future.

Our sensations influence our perceptions, which, in turn, affect our thoughts, emotions, and behaviors. If we feel cold, we put on a sweater. Likewise, if we feel pain, we typically reach for a pain reliever. The twist is: whether or not that pain reliever's effective often has nothing to do with the amount of medicine in it. Studies of the placebo effect show that many times fake cures work as well as real ones as long as we *believe* they do. "One region of the brain is activated by the expectation of pain relief," researchers tell CNN. "This, in turn, leads to a reduction of activity in the portion of the brain that senses pain."

In a parallel process called the "nocebo" effect, people taking placebo medications experience negative side effects or worse symptoms if they think the medicine's real and believe it will harm them. Cases like these reveal the complex nature of our senses and their intricate mind/body connections — links scientists are only beginning to understand.

MIND TINGLER

ATTENTION-GETTERS

What grabs our attention? Novelty and change, says Dr. A. James Hudspeth. "We tend to use our senses as an early warning system, so it's useful for our nervous system to filter out continuous inputs and focus on anything that's novel." Our senses tire easily with the same old stimuli.

Riding a roller coaster for the first time? Your heart races. You grip the lap bar, and your eyes fix straight ahead as you drop, dive, twist, turn, and barrel down the track at seventy-five miles an hour. After about the fifth ride, however, you're likely smiling and throwing your arms up in the air, because you've acclimated to the sensations.

Adaptations such as these illustrate how our senses not only mediate our perceptions of the world, but also filter and distort them. "What we perceive through our

Novelty and change excite our senses, which become easily bored with familiar input.

© AP Wide World Photos

senses is quite different from the physical characteristics of the stimuli around us," writes Maya Pines in "Seeing, Hearing, and Smelling the World." "We cannot see light in the ultraviolet range, though bees can, and we cannot detect light in the infrared range, though rattlesnakes can. Our nervous system reacts only to a selected range of wavelengths, vibrations, or other properties. It is limited by our genes, as well as our previous experience, and our current state of mind."

Our senses capture energy—from the eyes, ears, nose, skin, and tongue—and convert that energy into electrical signals that the brain or nervous system can interpret, explains Dr. Hudspeth. "During that conversion, there's always a certain amount of filtering or distortion because the external world has to be represented as an electrical signal."

Filtering often prevents information overload and keeps us focused on what's important. "The sensory receptors in our ears, for example, constantly work to throw away noise in the environment that's not selectively advantageous," says Dr. Hudspeth. That's why, when we talk on the phone with friends, we generally tune out any hissing or disruptive background sounds and hear only the speakers' voices.

Genes influence the sensory information we receive, as well. People born with congenital anosmia can't smell odors—fragrant or foul—which may affect their appetites, moods, and memories. About fifteen percent of us are "blind" to particular odors, including isobutyric acid, which is the smell of dirty socks.

THE SIXTH SENSE

Annette Martin says she "sees" dead people — an unusual skill that thrust her into the crime-solving field more than thirty years ago. One day while meditating in a yoga class, she had a vision. "I saw this body hanging horizontally above me," she recalls. "It was laying on something . . . and it was female, and she was dead."

"We have to go down to the police department," said her secretary after Annette shared her vision. "Maybe you've seen a murder that just happened."

"Are you nuts?" countered Annette, who worked as a psychic by day. "They're going to think I'm crazy." Worse yet, she worried police would think she was involved in a crime. Despite her doubts, Annette met with officers at the Marin County sheriff's department in California and was interrogated for hours. One detective who questioned her was Richard Keaton. He noticed that some of Annette's information matched unpublished details of a current murder investigation. Keaton brought Annette various objects associated with the case, including a set of keys, which she held and "read" for clues about the items and their owners — a psychic practice called psychometry. Annette also put herself in a trancelike state, which she says allowed her to travel "back to the murder scene."

"I went back to where this guy had picked the girl up. And [I] picked up on conversations, and then saw where he drove, described his car, described her, described him in detail . . . ," she says. Among other things, Annette told police that the suspect had stomach troubles and kept putting items into his mouth. Ultimately, she said, the case would take a year to solve and that the killer would be located "out of state" and "wearing white."

One year later, "to the day," they found him, says Annette. The suspect was working in the state of Washington "in a hospital and wearing white." When detectives searched his apartment, they discovered hundreds of antacid tablets — medicine used to relieve heartburn and stomach problems.

BEYOND BELIEF?

Stories like Annette's make many scientists and skeptics cringe. While the scenarios may be fascinating, they say, the dramatic tales feed the belief in the paranormal — experiences beyond the norm that defy our current scientific laws and understanding of the world. Newspaper articles featuring psychic detectives, television shows highlighting ghosts, and celebrities recounting "past lives" all seemingly add to the evidence, says social psychologist Thomas Gilovich in his book, *How We Know What Isn't So.* Even more persuasive are our own unusual experiences — dreams that seem to come true, and long-lost friends who call when we think about them.

A lot of personal experiences seem to teach us that paranormal phenomena are true, says Gilovich. "But appearances are deceptive sometimes, and this is one of those times. When someone has their back turned to us, and we're thinking thoughts about them — good or bad — and they suddenly turn around, it may seem like we've somehow created that. A lot of things seem like action at a distance," he says. "It's a very compelling feeling." An example is when you're playing cards and wishing for an ace of clubs and you get it. "The correlation between your intention and your activity and the outcome is such that it makes it seem like you caused it."

"A lot of things seem like action at a distance," says psychologist Thomas Gilovich. It's compelling to wish for an ace when you're playing cards and immediately get it.

© C. L. Jackson Images

Another reason people believe, he says, is because it's "quite inviting" and taps into our sense of awe and mystery. "A lot of skeptics say, 'Oh, the world is every bit as amazing without any sort of paranormal phenomena — I actually prefer it this way.' But I don't buy that. . . . The truth is, it *would* be amazing if we had those powers. However wonderful this world is, it'd be even more wonderful if that stuff were true. And that's partly what's responsible for why it sells so well. Who wouldn't want to believe that you can solve crimes by going deep into the mind and having some impressions that would help you do it?"

Perhaps these feelings explain why a 2005 Gallup poll found nearly three out of four Americans believe in at least one aspect of the paranormal. Thirty-seven percent of those polled believe houses can be haunted; 32 percent believe in ghosts and "that spirits of dead people can come back in certain places [or] situations"; and 25 percent believe in astrology, "or that the position of the stars and planets can affect people's lives."

Most popular is a belief in ESP, or extrasensory perception—also referred to as the sixth sense. ESP is a general term describing ways of knowing and acquiring information—from the past, present, and/or future—said to occur apart from our normally recognized senses. Among the most studied forms of ESP are telepathy, communicating thoughts and messages mind to mind; clairvoyance, sensing remote events, such as a distant friend's illness; and precognition, knowing information about events before they occur, such as accidents and natural disasters.

PROPHETIC VISIONS

People have always wondered about ESP and paranormal powers. Can fortunetellers predict the future by reading palms, gazing into crystal balls, or interpreting important numbers in our lives? Do spirits of

People have always wondered about the future and employed a variety of tools to help them predict what's ahead — such as tarot cards and crystal balls. Fortune-tellers also read palms, faces, and even moles to forecast a person's fate.

© Photodisc/Getty Images

the dead live on, and is it possible to communicate with them through mediums? Are a special few endowed with the gift of mind over matter — called psychokinesis — and can they will objects to bend and levitate?

One of the most famous forecasters of the future was a sixteenth-century Frenchman named Michel de Nostredame — more popularly known as Nostradamus. Born in 1503, Nostradamus spent his early years learning math, astrology, and languages from his grandfather and eventually studied the arts and medicine in college. Initially praised for his success in treating plague victims, Nostradamus turned to soothsaying later in his career. His most famous collection of prophecies, published in a work called *Centuries*, contains 942 predictions that are mostly grouped in hundreds. These visions — written in vague four-line verses called quatrains — include predictions about the end of the world and continue to be interpreted today.

Followers of Nostradamus credit him with predicting world

events ranging from the Great Fire of London and the French Revolution to the rise and fall of Hitler and the death of President John F. Kennedy. Skeptics, however, say any links rest in the eyes of interpreters who creatively connect the dots after events occur.

A few hundred years after Nostradamus, in the 1860s, the "spirit" photography of Boston engraver William H. Mumler captured people's imaginations. These unusual photographs not only recorded the images of clients, but also appeared to pick up ghostly reflections of their dead relatives and friends.

One of Mumler's most famous portraits is of Mary Todd Lincoln with an apparition of her late husband, President Abraham Lincoln, standing behind her. At the time, many welcomed the images as ethereal evidence.

Instead, they turned out to be products of darkroom deception: Mumler and other spirit photographers had doubly exposed film and superimposed ghostly figures on the originals.

Today, researchers who study paranormal abilities — called

In this portrait of Mary Todd Lincoln, taken by William H. Mumler, her late husband, President Abraham Lincoln, appears to be standing behind her with his hands resting on her shoulders.

Courtesy of the Lincoln Museum, Fort Wayne, Indiana

parapsychologists — continue to battle frauds and struggle for credibility. However, they're working to gain respect by testing various psychic phenomena in the lab to try to establish its existence under carefully controlled experiments more in line with mainstream science. This is how "we separate bizarre ideas from those that sound bizarre but are true," reminds psychologist David G. Myers.

One popular test for ESP conducted at the Rhine Research Center in North Carolina is called the ganzfeld (German for "whole field") technique. During the experiment, two people in isolated rooms attempt to mentally send and receive information to and from each other. In one room, a "receiver" sits with ping-pong-ball halves over his eyes, looks into a red light, and listens to waterfall-like noises through headphones. "The goal is to create an altered state of consciousness," says John Palmer, director of research. The environment is designed to make a person's "thought processes more spontaneous and to allow them to focus their attention inward, where they can pick up subtle impressions." Once in an altered state, the receiver reports aloud "anything and everything that pops into his or her mind" in an attempt to identify the content of a randomly selected picture or movie clip that the "sender" is trying to transmit from another room.

After about a half hour, the receiver is shown four possible pictures or movie clips and asked to choose the one most closely matching their mental imagery during the experiment. "By chance, they're going to do that correctly twenty-five percent of the time," explains Palmer. "And in our laboratory — and in other laboratories — they found that the average is about thirty-three percent, which [is] . . . quite significant statistically," he says.

Not everyone who has analyzed the data agrees with Palmer's enthusiastic evaluation, leaving the issue open to further debate. One of those researchers is Richard Wiseman, a psychology professor at the University of Hertfordshire in England. Wiseman began his career as a professional magician and now studies topics such as the psychology of deception, psychic fraud, and the paranormal. He believes it's important to rule out fraud in parapsychology to keep people from being hurt emotionally, physically, and/or financially. One case he cites points to a young man who killed himself after a psychic told him he would be dead by age twenty-eight.

GHOSTLY MATTERS

Ever felt ghoulish sensations while visiting a castle or a "haunted" house? It could be that you're unconsciously tapping into infrasound — sound pitched too low for humans to hear, but which we can sometimes feel. Wiseman and an acoustic scientist conducted an experiment at a London concert hall where they played contemporary music — some mixed with infrasound, some not — and asked the audience of 750 to describe their reactions. Twenty-two percent reported strange experiences, including feelings of intense sorrow, nervousness, and spine-tingling chills. Wiseman explains that "some scientists have suggested that this level of sound may be present at some allegedly haunted sites and so cause people to have odd sensations that they attribute to a ghost. Our findings support these ideas," he says.

Some people believe the fifth floor of this Reno County Courthouse in Hutchinson, Kansas, is haunted by a ghost named Lily, who plays with the lights and cries out at night. They say she hanged herself in the jail, which was once located on the fifth floor.

© AP Wide World Photos

In another experiment, Wiseman and colleague Emma Greening developed a "Mind Machine" to test people's ability to predict the outcome of a random coin toss. If people possessed the power to influence the toss, they'd call it correctly — heads or tails — more than fifty percent of the time. Using a touch-screen computer, visitors answered several questions — including whether or not they believed in psychic abilities. They then had four opportunities to make their calls. After touring museums, science festivals, and shopping centers throughout Britain, the Mind Machine collected more than "a quarter of a million datapoints," reports Wiseman. Results, he says, "did not reveal any evidence to support the existence of extrasensory perception."

Wiseman also failed to find proof that psychic sleuths outperform the average person when it comes to helping solve crimes. In 1994, he led a study comparing the skills of three British psychic detectives with those of three college students for a television documentary. Participants were given three items associated with three solved crimes. After holding the items, they were asked to share any "thoughts, images, and ideas" that came to mind relating to the cases. Later they were asked to pick six statements out of eighteen that they believed applied to each crime. "Results from this formal test revealed that the psychics were no more accurate than the students, and that neither group performed at above chance levels."

Wiseman also noted that while the students didn't think they performed well on the task, the psychics believed they were "very successful." In addition, one psychic overlooked his incorrect statements. "This lends support to the notion that some psychic detection may appear to work, in part, because inaccurate predictions may be forgotten about whereas successful ones are recalled and elaborated upon."

ANIMAL SUPER SENSES

Hours before the earth buckled and triggered one of the most deadly series of tsunamis in history on December 26, 2004, animals along the Indian Ocean's affected coastline seemed to sense danger. Elephants trumpeted. Dolphins dashed for deeper waters. Flamingos flew to higher ground, and bats roused from their usual daytime slumber. When it was over, more than 225,000 people died or went missing. Surprisingly, few animals perished. "We have not found any dead animals along this part of the coast," the manager of Khao Lak National Park in Thailand told a reporter several days after the tragedy. He said they all ran high into the hills and had yet to return.

What saved the animals and prompted them to flee to safety? Was it a mysterious sixth sense? "I don't know if I'd call this a sixth sense so much as a better sense," Ken Grant of the Humane Society International Asia office told the *Washington Post*. "Most animals know that when the ground starts to shake, something is wrong."

Animals' extraordinary senses are well documented. Nature's stretched their sensory perception skills in all directions to help them survive — and thrive — in a wide range of environments.

•MIGRATORY BIRDS possess a magnetic sense that guides them to food and warmth south in the fall and north in the spring. Honeybees, sharks, sea turtles, salmon, and salamanders also benefit from built-in compasses.

•RATTLESNAKES sense the body heat of other animals. Using heat-sensing organs on the sides of their head called loreal pits, they can "see" heat images of prey that are fractions of a degree warmer than their environment — day or night.

•BATS navigate their surroundings by emitting high-pitched sounds and interpreting the echoes. This radarlike sense — called echolocation — helps them detect the size, location, and movements of prey.

•ELECTRIC EELS stun their prey and defend themselves by producing currents as high as 650 volts. The eels, which are actually knifefish, also use their electrical senses to orient themselves in water and communicate with each other.

Honeybees and humans live in different sensory worlds. While bees can see light in the ultraviolet range, humans cannot.
Courtesy of the U.S. Department of Agriculture

Many people believe similar "super senses" enable animals to read nature's warning signs before disasters such as earthquakes, hurricanes, volcanoes, and tsunamis. Countless reports exist of unusual behavior by animals — from dogs and cows to bees and jellyfish — in the hours and days before a disaster. Some animals wail, act aggressively, or become nervous and disoriented. Others panic and run. One Japanese legend tells of a giant catfish that lives beneath the earth and makes the ground tremble with its every move. "The legend probably derives from the unusual behavior — violent jumping and twisting movements — that has been observed in catfish before earthquakes," explains Motoji Ikeya, a retired geophysics professor at Osaka University in Japan and author of *Earthquakes and Animals: From Folk Legends to Science.*

PROPHETIC HISTORY

Stories of animals sensing oncoming catastrophes date back centuries. Historians recount that days before an earthquake swallowed the Greek city of Helice in 373 B.C.E., countless worms emerged from their burrows and scores of snakes, rats, and weasels deserted the region. Birds, mice, and other animals also reportedly escaped the massive quake of 1775 in Lisbon, Portugal, which killed as many as 60,000 people.

More recently, geologist Jim Berkland predicted the October 1989 "World Series Quake" that shook the San Francisco Bay area based primarily on the abnormally high number of missing cats and dogs before the disaster — information he gleaned from local newspaper ads for lost pets. In the port city of Kobe, Japan, reports collected after a catastrophic 1995 quake revealed curious early distress signals from animals. Sea lions "cried, refused to eat, jumped about, swam in zigzag, and fussed," say zookeepers. Crocodiles "clawed violently at the glass walls of their enclosure" and "hippos submerged themselves before the quake and refused to surface for three days."

Can monitoring animal behaviors help us predict earthquakes? Many scientists remain skeptical — if only for practical reasons. Not only are animal activities difficult to replicate in a lab, they say, other variables must be considered — such as location differences and individual animal responses. For example, while eyewitnesses reported elephants fleeing for higher ground before the Indian Ocean tsunami, two satellite-collared elephants in Yala National Park off Sri Lanka's coast hardly moved. One actually headed for the beach, instead of inland.

According to researchers at the United States Geological Survey (USGS), whose mission is to study the earth and minimize loss of life and property from natural disasters:

Changes in animal behavior cannot be used to predict earthquakes. Even though there have been documented cases of unusual animal behavior prior to earthquakes, a reproducible connection between a specific behavior and the occurrence of an earthquake has not been made. Because of their finely tuned senses, animals can often feel the earthquake at its earliest stages before the humans around it can. This feeds the myth that the animal knew the earthquake was coming. But animals also change their behavior for many reasons, and given that an earthquake can shake millions of people, it is likely that a few [animals/pets] will, by chance, be acting strangely before an earthquake.

Despite such assertions, some researchers worldwide believe enough anecdotal evidence exists to pursue studies and heed animal omens. In 1971, for instance, the Chinese government began collecting reports of odd animal behavior as an aid to predict earthquakes. "Four years later, based on observations of unusual animal behavior and geophysical measurements, they successfully evacuated Haicheng city several hours before an earthquake on February 4, 1975," explains Ikeya. The evacuation is estimated to have saved as many as 100,000 lives. Scientists later discovered that foreshocks — small tremors before a major quake — may have bolstered the prediction. Still, say supporters, the incident shows earthquakes sometimes send signals before they strike — signs that may alert animals and potentially save lives.

NATURAL REACTIONS

What, if anything, could animals be sensing?

Bill Barklow, a biologist who studies hippo communications, doesn't believe hippos or other animals evolve special adaptations for avoiding tsunamis and earthquakes. Instead, he thinks it's possible some animals may respond to low frequency rumblings associated with thunderstorms and natural disasters, called infrasounds. Humans can't hear sounds in this range, but animals that do — such as giraffes, elephants, and tigers — may be frightened by them. In fact, hippos send out infrasonic "bubble blasts" when they want to threaten and intimidate others, says Barklow. Perhaps the animals equate infrasound with danger.

Hippos build up large amounts of pressure under their nostrils before sending out infrasonic "bubble blasts," which are sounds they use to threaten and intimidate others.

© AP Wide World Photos

Another possibility is that some animals sense ground vibrations rippling through the Earth's surface hours before quakes and tsunamis. "Known as Rayleigh waves [for Lord Rayleigh, who predicted their existence in 1885], these vibrations move through the ground like waves move on the surface of the ocean," reports Christine Kenneally. Not only do they travel at about "ten times the speed of sound," but a variety of animals can detect them, including some insects, birds, and mammals. Elephants, for example, may sense these seismic signals through special receptors in their feet and trunks, says Caitlin

O'Connell-Rodwell, a Stanford University researcher and author of *The Elephant's Secret Sense*. "Often, you'll see a whole group that freezes," she says. During this synchronized freezing, the elephants stop mid-stride, lean forward, and stand as still as statues while placing additional weight on their front feet. Some will even lift a foot to add extra weight on the other or lay their trunks flat, she explains. "It's a focusing posture so they can really pay attention to what they're feeling on the ground."

A third possible warning may come from electrical signals, says Japanese researcher Motoji Ikeya. Rocks—particularly granite and quartz grain deposits—undergo increased pressure before an earthquake and release electromagnetic energy, which he suspects some animals detect. To test his theory, Ikeya conducted humane lab experiments* with a variety of animals so he could gauge their sensitivity to electromagnetic pulses. Electrodes were placed in aquariums, for instance, to run carefully measured electrical pulses in tanks containing fish and other aquatic animals. When testing worms, he attached

Scientists believe elephants lay their trunks flat on the ground to help them focus and detect low-frequency communications from distant herds. Some think this may be how elephants seem to sense earthquakes before humans feel them.

© Corbis

*Ikeya reports no animals were harmed or killed during the experiments.

electrodes to "opposite ends of a box containing wet soil." Ultimately, Ikeya's findings echoed many people's descriptions of animal behavior prior to earthquakes: bees became agitated; earthworms surfaced from the soil; and the generally quiet catfish — naturally equipped with electrosensory organs to detect prey — jerked violently.

Ikeya's now convinced there's "a scientific basis to many of the legendary and reported precursors" to earthquakes. However, he also believes animals alone aren't the answer. Using technology to monitor changes in electromagnetic fields — along with observing animals such as catfish — would be most reliable, he says. Taking these steps "should permit a rough estimate to be made of the likely region, time, and magnitude of a large quake."

RUNAWAY SHARKS

Just as some animals appear to read cryptic clues preceding earthquakes, others seem to sense incoming storms. Seven hours before Tropical Storm Gabrielle slammed Florida's Gulf coast on September 13, 2001, thirteen electronically tagged blacktip sharks in a nursery near Tampa Bay swam for deeper waters only to return two weeks later. A similar pattern occurred when Hurricane Charley hit the region in August 2004, says Michelle Heupel, a staff scientist at the Mote Marine Laboratory in Sarasota, Florida.

To determine why the sharks left the area so suddenly, Heupel examined environmental variables. "I looked at wind speed, and it didn't go up any more than it would during a summer storm," she

As Hurricane Charley approached the Florida Coast in September 2004, sharks fitted with acoustic transmitters, such as the one pictured above, swam for deeper waters.

Courtesy of Michelle R. Heupel, Mote Marine Laboratory

says. The tides were normal and the rainfall didn't peak until after the animals had left, so they weren't factors. Heupel then looked at barometric pressure and noticed the sharks abandoned the nursery at about the same time the pressure began dropping. The marine scientist suspects a connection.

"Sharks have pressure sensors in their ears," she explains. "As the air pressure decreases, there's less pressure on the water surface, which means the water pressure changes as well." Sharks who feel safe swimming in five feet of water may now feel as if they're in a shallow three feet. Heupel believes this may prompt them to move to deeper waters before a storm.

DOG IN THE HOUSE?

Closer to home, man's best friends are engaging in some serious sniffing.

When Debbie Marvit-McGlothin was about four months pregnant, her dog, Autumn, began licking at a dark brown mole she'd developed on the back of her left thigh. "I didn't think anything of it at the time," she says, "because I have lots of moles." But Autumn persisted. When Debbie returned home from her night shift as a nurse, Autumn licked the mole. When Debbie slept during the day, Autumn licked the mole. "She'd lick it all day long," recalls Debbie. As the weeks rolled by, the two-year-old shepherd-hound mix grew more aggressive, scratching and biting at the site.

Debbie mentioned Autumn's mole obsession to her doctor. "We can remove it if you'd like," he told her, which she did to play it safe. A few weeks later, Debbie learned the mole was melanoma — a severe form of skin cancer that can turn fatal if allowed to spread. "I was

shocked," says Debbie, who admits she really didn't believe "in things like this" until it happened to her. "I wouldn't have even known I had a mole there if Autumn didn't go at it nonstop. The fact that she sniffed the cancer out is pretty amazing."

Dogs pack a pretty powerful snout. While humans smell the world with about five million sensory cells, dogs sniff it using anywhere from 125 to 220 million — one reason we train them to find everything from explosives to missing persons. With stories like

When Debbie Marvit-McGlothin's dog Autumn wouldn't stop sniffing at a mole she'd developed on the back of her left thigh, she had it removed. Not long after, she learned the mole was cancerous.

Courtesy of Debbie Marvit-McGlothin

Debbie's circulating, some wondered if dogs could be taught to sniff out cancer. Scientists at the Pine Street Foundation in California decided to find out.

"Much of our research focuses on early-detection methods for cancer," explains Nicholas Broffman, executive director of the foundation. "And dogs are one of those methods." Working with five "ordinary" young canines — three Labrador retrievers and two Portuguese water dogs — scientists set out to determine if dogs could be trained to detect lung and breast cancer from samples of people's breath.

What they found astonished them. After about three weeks of training, the dogs identified lung cancer breath samples with 99 percent accuracy and breast cancer samples with 88 percent accuracy. "Gone are the days when somebody could completely dismiss the idea," says Broffman. The results "suggest that more research in the field is necessary." Cancer experts agree. Dogs detecting cancer is "not crazy at all," Dr. Ted Gansler of the American Cancer Society told the New York Times. "It's biologically plausible," he says, "but there has to be a lot more study and confirmation of effectiveness."

Just as important is evidence that cancers "hidden deep within the body" may be detected through a person's breath, say Pine Street Foundation researchers. The group's now working with scientists at the University of Maine to pinpoint any chemicals the dogs may have detected in cancer patients' breath. Ultimately, their goal is to develop a cancer version of an "electronic nose." The device would work much like a Breathalyzer — a tool that police use to measure the amount of alcohol consumed by drunk drivers — and could be used in doctors' offices to prescreen for cancer.

"The dog's brain and nose is currently one of the most sophisticated odor detection devices on the planet," say the researchers. "Technology now has to rise to meet that challenge."

MIND TINGLER

SENSE-SATIONS

HAIR RAISERS: Ever break out in **goose bumps** when you're feeling cold, scared, or inspired? Those little bumps are caused by tiny muscles at the base of your body hairs that contract and lift up each hair. No one knows exactly why they occur, but scientists think they may have evolved as part of our fight-or-flight response to perceived threats.

LYING EYES: Gaze at a single star or planet in a dark night sky and it will soon appear to bounce around. Scientists call this illusion the **autokinetic effect**. Many believe it happens because we perceive motion in relationship to other objects, and when there are no reference points or background cues, the movement of the star or planet becomes difficult to determine. The autokinetic effect is thought to be one reason people mistake stars and planets for unidentified flying objects (UFOs).

EMOTIONAL SCENTS: Popcorn. Baby powder. Freshly baked bread. Mention any of these items and they'll trigger fond memories for most people. Smelling them, however, will evoke even more emotionally vivid memories and increase your heart rate, according to Rachel Herz, a psychology professor and researcher at Brown University. Our sense of smell is intricately linked to our memories. "The olfactory nerve synapses almost directly into the amygdala, which is responsible for emotional experience and also human emotional memory," says Herz. She notes that from an evolutionary standpoint, the emotional centers of our brain "grew out of the olfactory area, so it's possible that if we didn't have the sense of smell, we might not have emotion."

INTUITION:
MORE THAN A FEELING

new neighbor. You've barely met, but you've got a funny feeling you'll be great friends. Maybe it's her warm smile or quirky mannerisms. Perhaps you're charmed by her obvious love of animals: three dogs, two cats, and several guinea pigs. Whatever it is, you're sure things will work out. Your intuition — or immediate sense of knowing — is telling you so.

Chances are you can trust your instincts. Research shows our first impressions can be remarkably accurate in judging certain personality traits and skills. In one study, it took only a matter of seconds for students to form an impression — positive or negative — about professors' teaching abilities and accurately predict their ratings at the end of the college semester.

Scientists say we have "two minds." Our rational mind is deliberate and conscious. It gathers facts, evaluates situations, and logically develops solutions over time. Our intuitive mind, on the other hand, is fast, automatic, and unconscious. It works below the surface and instantly picks up and judges all sorts of information without us knowing it.

Some think our intuitive reflexes are time-saving "mental shortcuts" or "rules of thumb" (called heuristics) that we use to interpret the world. For example, the "recognition heuristic" says that when in doubt, go with what you recognize — and that's what many of us instinctively do. Others believe our inner voices stem from learned associations based on life experiences. "Intuition is just the things we've learned without realizing we've learned them," says psychologist Seymour Epstein. A string of positive relationships with people will probably yield a different "social intuition" than a history of bad experiences, he says. Likewise, we may instinctively fear

Studies show that our first impressions of people can be remarkably accurate in judging some—but not all—personality traits and skills.

© JUPITERIMAGES

strangers who remind us of a person who has hurt us in the past or instantly feel close to someone who resembles a best friend.

Malcolm Gladwell, author of *Blink: The Power of Thinking Without Thinking*, attributes much of our intuition — or "rapid cognition" as he prefers to call it — to "thin-slicing." The term "refers to the ability of our unconscious to find patterns in situations and behaviors based on very narrow slices of experiences," he explains. "We thin-slice whenever we meet a new person or have to make sense of something quickly. We thin-slice because we have to, and we come to rely on that ability because there are lots of . . . situations where careful attention to the details of a very thin slice, even for no more than a second or two, can tell us an awful lot."

BEHIND CLOSED DOORS

Want to learn more about a person? Spend fifteen minutes in their bedroom when they're not around, says psychologist Sam Gosling at the University of Texas at Austin. Bedrooms, offices, and other personal spaces are rich with clues about people's values, lifestyle, and personality, he says. In one study, Gosling and fellow researchers sent people to the bedrooms of eighty-three strangers and asked them to answer questions about the occupants based on their initial impressions. Then they compared the impressions with personality reports from close friends. While close friends were best at judging how outgoing and good-natured people were based on their relationships, strangers who thin-sliced bedrooms proved more accurate in three out of five areas: openness, conscientiousness, and emotionally stability.

"You learn different things from different contexts," Gosling says. "If you want to know how extroverted people are, you should meet them, and you can figure it out in five minutes." If you want to know how conscientious they are, you should look at their bedrooms. The rooms will be "very neat, organized, and tidy — just as you'd expect," he says. Their bookshelves may even be alphabetized.

Bedrooms also reveal people's openness to new experiences as

If you want to learn more about a person, spend fifteen minutes in his or her bedroom when they're not around, says psychologist Sam Gosling.

© Unlisted Images, Inc.

well as "how broadminded, imaginative, and creative they are," says Gosling. The biggest clue to openness is how distinctively the space is decorated, he says. It shows a person's creativity. A broad and unique range of reading materials and music also signal an open mind.

How can strangers intuitively read so much from a room?

Gosling believes we pick up on traces of people's personalities woven into their environments. "Every single element, every item, got here somehow," he says, pointing to three ways we generally leave personal breadcrumbs. The first — and most obvious — are "identity claims," he says, noting that there are two types. *Other-directed* identity claims are items such as flags people hang to convey their values and goals. "A great example is a poster on the outside of a door. The person who occupies the space can't see it, but everyone else can," he says. In contrast, *self-directed* identity claims are items you can see, such as mouse pads and screen-savers with sayings, symbols, or images that reinforce your beliefs, but which others may not necessarily understand.

Another type of personality clue we unconsciously leave in our wake is *behavioral residue*, says Gosling. "My desk is not messy because I deliberately want to give people that impression, it's messy as a consequence of my behavior — not putting things back where they belong." A person with to-do lists everywhere might inadvertently tell the world she's feeling overwhelmed, while a racing bib and sneakers may reveal her love of running.

A third way people project their personalities is through *thought and feeling regulators* — items we surround ourselves with to create particular moods. A room may overflow with candles, plants, and pillows to promote relaxation or be clutter-free to minimize distractions. What's missing also may speak volumes. Photos of everyone but a brother may reveal a rocky relationship. No photos could mean the person's reserved or not the sentimental type.

All these factors affect people's impressions, says Gosling. But they need to be taken in context. "You can't really say that this clue means this, and this clue means that. There's no one-to-one relationship. It's really a configuration of things. The meaning of one thing modifies the meaning of another."

The concept works similarly for personal Web pages, where people create virtual images for social networking, and for music preferences, which offer unique clues to our personalities, says Gosling. "Just as the social and physical environments that people select and shape reflect their personalities . . . so too do their musical environments," he says. "Cheerful music," for example, is associated with extroverts; "vigorous" music with athletes. People also use music to associate themselves with certain groups and to "send a message to others about who they are or how they like to be seen," explains Gosling. Those who view themselves as "intellectual," for instance, "might listen to complex music (such as classical and jazz) because it projects an image of sophistication."

People who view themselves as "intellectual" often listen to complex music such as classical and jazz, say researchers.

© JUPITERIMAGES

Sound a little like stereotyping? After analyzing personality and music preferences from more than 10,000 people worldwide, Gosling and social psychologist Jason Rentfrow say "there does (seem) to be a kernel of truth to at least some of the music stereotypes. This isn't to say that everyone who likes one style of music has exactly the same personality and music preferences," they add. "Instead, it means that, *on average,* people who like one style of music *more often than not* display similar personality characteristics and tend to like similar types of music. We're talking about generalizations here," they emphasize, "and these generalizations don't apply to all people."

SPEED BUMPS

The same principle holds true for generalizations we use as intuitive cues to understand the world. While they're often reliable, they can sometimes lead us astray, says psychologist David G. Myers, author of *Intuition: Its Powers and Perils.* "Thanks to pathways that run from the eye to the brain's emotional control centers — bypassing the cortex — we often feel before we analyze," he says. When those feelings are rooted in unconscious biases or preconceived notions, they can throw off our judgments.

"Before classical musicians were routinely auditioned behind screens, it was believed women couldn't play as well as men," writes Gladwell in *Blink.*

They didn't have the strength, the attitude, or the resilience for certain kinds of pieces. Their lips were different. Their lungs less powerful. Their hands were smaller. That did not seem like a prejudice. It seemed like a fact, because when conductors and music directors and maestros held auditions, the men always seemed to sound better than the women.

Thirty years and a few blind auditions later, he says, more women are playing in "top U.S. orchestras" than ever before.

"We have biases—every one of us," says Mahazarin Banaji, a social ethics professor at Harvard University. Banaji is one of the creators of the Implicit Association Test (www.implicit.harvard.edu/implicit/), a research tool that gives people the opportunity to uncover and examine their hidden stereotypes and prejudices. Test-takers are asked to pair words with various faces as quickly as possible. The faster a person matches two items—say the face of a young person and the word "good"—the stronger the automatic or implicit bond.

Results from more than four and a half million tests reveal most participants unknowingly hold negative attitudes toward some groups of people in contrast to their professed beliefs. For example, researchers report that more than 80 percent of Americans who took the test on the Web "show implicit negativity toward the elderly compared to the young." They say such underlying feelings can unwittingly influence everything from friendships to work evaluations and contribute to job discrimination—one reason to resist and challenge some of our snap judgments.

Intuition also shapes many of our fears, which is another reason to be careful, says Myers. "Why do so many smokers—whose habits shorten their lives, on average, by about five years—fret before flying, which averaged across people, shortens life by one day? Why do we fear tragic but isolated terrorist attacks more than . . . global climate change?" Our instincts tell us to, Myers says. Plane rides are "immediate," and global warming is in the distant future. By acknowledging intuition's limits and balancing it with rational thought, he says, we can make smarter decisions.

In fact, experts balance analytical and intuitive thinking all the time, enabling them to sharpen their instincts. "Basketball is an intricate, high-speed game filled with split-second, spontaneous decisions," notes Gladwell. "But that spontaneity is possible only when everyone first engages in hours of highly repetitive and structured practice . . . *spontaneity isn't random,*" he says. "How good people's decisions are under the fast-moving, high-stress conditions of rapid cognition is a function of training and rules and rehearsal."

Expert Timing

Intuition begins with recognizing a situation, says Gary Klein, a psychologist and author who studies highly experienced firefighters, pilots, chess masters, and others who make decisions under extreme time pressure. He and his colleagues have "estimated that fireground commanders make around eighty percent of their decisions in less than one minute." They've also "studied chess

Intuition helps expert chess players and other professionals "size up a situation" and quickly develop a plan of action based on past experiences, says psychologist Gary Klein.

© JUPITERIMAGES

players under blitz conditions, where the average move was made in six seconds."

Klein's found that intuition helps experts "size up a situation" quickly and almost instantly create an action plan based on knowledge gained from past experiences. They're then able to promptly evaluate and refine decisions by imagining scenarios and how they'll play out. Such intuitive expertise is not limited to emergency situations, says Klein. We all use it in areas where we've accumulated knowledge and experiences that hone our judgments—whether it's driving a car or playing video games.

Jo-Ellan Dimitrius, author of *Reading People*, applies her know-how when helping to select juries for trials. In minutes, she forms an initial impression of people based on factors such as their interests, body language, and most striking traits. As she collects more information, Dimitrius adjusts her impressions.

In one case involving a man on trial for murder, she writes, all facts pointed to dismissing a prospective juror. Why then did her intuition tell her the person might have an open mind?

The answer became apparent on the second day of questioning. Unlike most jurors who walk around defendants charged with violent crimes as they navigate through the courtroom, the young woman looked his way and walked right by him, she says. "While I had not consciously registered that this woman's behavior was dramatically unusual, my subconscious had raised a flag." The behavior told Dimitrius the woman "was not afraid of the man, as most jurors would be if they had already judged him guilty of murder." A good sign for the defense.

COINCIDENCES:
TWISTS OF FATE OR FLUKES?

One thing is certain about coincidence. The phenomenon fascinates believers and skeptics alike. It's a porthole into one of the most interesting philosophical questions. . . . Is there a deeper order, an overarching purpose to the universe? Or are we the lucky accidents of evolution, living our precious but brief lives in a fundamentally random world that has only the meaning we choose to give it?

—Jill Neimark, "The Power of Coincidence," *Psychology today*

On the first anniversary of the September 11th terrorist attacks—often referred to as 9/11—the New York State Lottery's evening numbers rolled out the winning combination of 9-1-1. "A bizarre and eerie coincidence," marveled one reporter. "Chilling," said others. What were the odds that those particular numbers would be drawn in New York on that particular day?

Not as unlikely as you might imagine, says Karl Sigman, a professor in the department of operations research at Columbia University in New York whose research focuses on probability theory — a branch of mathematics that models and analyzes uncertainty and randomness.

"This New York lottery game is played twice each day, so that means there are seven hundred and thirty chances [365 × 2] per year for the outcome to match the day," explains Sigman. "Each chance has a one in one thousand probability of matching, so there's about a fifty-two percent probability that within any given year, the outcome of the lottery will match the day. Moreover, on average, a match will occur about seven times during any given ten-year period." When this happens, he says, some people attach "special meaning" to the event — especially if it occurs on a day that's important to them, such as their birthday, or, in this case, the tragic day of September 11th. The numbers may have matched another day, he says, but people might have missed it because the day wasn't as significant to them.

Some believe otherwise.

"To rely on dry mathematics is to miss the philosophical and spiritual point," writes Sarah Gibb in *The Star Phoenix* newspaper of Saskatoon, Canada. "Because the astonishing fact is this — on one of the very few days in the history of our universe, and perhaps on the only day when literally every man and woman on the planet was probably thinking of the same thing and was watching images or reading words connected to that thing . . . the haunting numbers nine-eleven — those lottery balls 'thought' of them, too."

Gibb wondered if the energy generated by everyone's thoughts "somehow influenced the machine that dropped those particular balls into [their] tubes on that particular day?"

Others wondered as well — not only about the lottery numbers, but also about another incident on the morning of September 11, 2002. In an article titled, "A sudden breeze, and loved ones seem near," reporter Jessica McBride of the *Milwaukee Journal Sentinel* describes the scene.

NEW YORK—As the convoys of bagpipers took the first determined steps onto the hallowed field of dirt, and the families of the dead lifted pictures of their loved ones aloft, and the politicians solemnly lined up on a platform, a gust of wind suddenly swirled out of nowhere.

The skies over lower Manhattan had been calm earlier Wednesday, and robin's-egg blue. But the wind blew a halo of dust into the air over ground zero, just minutes before the Sept. 11 anniversary ceremony was about to begin.

It swirled throughout the nearly three-hour observance, like the faint echo of a year ago, when the heavy dust of two towering buildings and 2,801 bodies blanketed the area.

[One woman] who came Wednesday to mourn her brother . . . thought: this can't be a coincidence. Standing on the scarred plot of land where so many perished, the dust, to her, "symbolized life, even spirits in some way. . . ."

Dust swirled throughout the first September 11th anniversary ceremony at Ground Zero in New York. For some, it seemed more than a coincidence.

© AP Wide World Photos

Was the sudden squall of wind that came "out of nowhere" during the ceremony a sign? Did it carry a deeper meaning? Certainly for some, the incident signified more than a random weather glitch. The timing of the wind gusts may have represented a "meaningful coincidence" or what the late Swiss psychiatrist Carl Jung calls synchronicity.

Coincidences happen when two or more unusual events occur at about the same time and *"by chance are related to each other through some kind of noticeable similarity,"* writes psychotherapist Robert H. Hopcke in his book, *There Are No Accidents*. Synchronicity happens, he says, when a coincidental event means something special to a person—usually in an intensely emotional and symbolic way. Often, a synchronistic event signals a transition or turning point in a person's life.

"When Doris and I attended Texas Tech College, we were good friends and dated several months," explains Hollis Long. "Then she graduated in the spring and went back home to Holliday, Texas. I really thought I'd never see her again.

"One summer night, about two months later, I dreamed I was sitting in my apartment when I heard a knock at the door. I opened the door and Doris was standing outside. Then I woke up.

"That afternoon, I was actually sitting in my apartment when I heard a knock at the door. I opened the door, and there was Doris. She had come to Lubbock to attend a wedding and dropped by to visit me."

A dream coincidence kindled a romance between Hollis and Doris Long, who went on to marry and have four children together. From top left to right: Rebecca, Arthur, Bruce, and Hollis; at bottom, Valerie and Doris.

Courtesy of Hollis E. Long

Hollis's experience rekindled a courtship that eventually led to marriage. It helped him "make sense of his world" and became an integral part of his life story — something Hopcke says is an important role of synchronicity. The couple went on to become the parents of four children and the grandparents of nine.

While some view Hollis's dream coincidence as synchronicity, others see it as a nudge from a higher power. SQuire Rushnell, author of *When God Winks: How the Power of Coincidence Guides Your Life,* would probably call Hollis's dream a "God Wink," something he defines as "a personal signal or message, directly from a higher power," that usually happens as a coincidence. Rushnell believes these winks are signs meant to reassure us that we're moving in the right direction along life's path.

Similarly, Joan Wester Anderson, who has written many books about guardian angels, would probably view Hollis's experience as a sign from the heavens that his relationship with Doris was something special. Perhaps his guardian angel was playing matchmaker.

Anderson first became interested in angels when her son, Tim, and his college friends were rescued by a mysterious tow-truck driver one dangerously cold Christmas Eve. After towing the boys and their car to safety, the stranger disappeared without a trace, she says. Anderson checked into the situation with city officials. She learned that a curfew had been imposed because of the bitter cold and that no tow trucks had been sent out during the night in question. To this day, whoever helped her son and his friends in their time of need remains a mystery.

COINCIDENTAL CONNECTIONS

Our brains are wired to make cause-and-effect connections, so when something out of the ordinary happens — such as a coincidence — we immediately look for explanations. What we find — our interpretations of the situation — often depends on our background knowledge and experiences, says Josh Tenenbaum, a cognitive scientist at the Massachusetts Institute of Technology (MIT). Tenenbaum studies coincidences to learn more about how the mind comes to understand the world given the limited information it receives through our senses.

Coincidences represent a true paradox, he says. "On the one hand they seem to be the source of our greatest irrationalities — seeing causal connections when science tells us they aren't there. On the other hand, some of our greatest feats of scientific discovery depend on coincidences."

The discovery of Halley's Comet is a great example, says Tenenbaum. After sifting through years of astronomical records, English astronomer Sir Edmond Halley noted a strange coincidence in 1705: "One comet seemed to appear in a particular part of the sky and travel in a particular direction at regular intervals of about seventy-five to seventy-six years."

Applying what he knew about Newton's laws of motion and planetary orbits, Halley theorized that the comets seen in 1531 and 1607, and one he had observed in 1682, were actually the same comet traveling in an elliptical orbit around the sun. From this, he predicted

Some of our greatest discoveries, such as the discovery of Halley's Comet, happen when people take note of coincidences and validate their theories with science.

© AP Wide World Photos

the comet's return in 1758. Halley didn't live to see it, but the comet reappeared on Christmas night of that year and later was named in his honor.

In a similar manner, Dr. John Snow noticed a curious coincidence during a severe outbreak of cholera that killed hundreds of Londoners in August 1854. "Snow immediately suspected a water pump on Broad Street as the cause, but could find little evidence of contamination," says Tenenbaum. "However, on collecting information about the locations of the cholera victims, he discovered that they were tightly clustered around the pump. This suspicious coincidence hardened his convictions, and the pump handle was removed." When the disease stopped spreading, it advanced Snow's theory that cholera was caused by contaminated water and not bad air, as many had previously believed.

Along with sparking scientific discovery, coincidences fuel children's learning. After seeing several examples of a horse, for instance, most preschoolers can identify the animal based on a cluster of common characteristics. "Somehow their mind is primed to look for certain kinds of coincidences in a few examples," says Tenenbaum. "And when they're given a label, such as horse, they think, 'Okay, so that's what the label means.' It's not like they always get it right, but when you think of all the logical possibilities, it's amazing how often they're correct in learning a new word or concept from just one or two examples."

On the flip side, too little information when interpreting coincidences also can lead to erroneous and superstitious beliefs, says Tenenbaum. Just as an optical illusion plays tricks with our visual senses, inadequate data can fool our brains into jumping to wrong conclusions about the world. The difference, he says, is that with an optical illusion, people can see how their eyes played tricks on them and move on with their lives. When they make judgments about the world based on faulty reasoning, however, it can influence their day-to-day thoughts and decisions and result in beliefs such as conspiracy theories.

"For example, during World War II London was struck by German V-1 flying bombs and V-2 rockets," explain Tenenbaum and Professor Tom Griffiths of the University of California, Berkeley. "The locations at which they landed seemed to cluster in poorer parts of the city, and there was a widespread belief that these areas were being specifically targeted. After the war, the locations where the flying bombs fell were subjected to statistical analysis. It showed that they had fallen uniformly at random. The apparent clustering that people had perceived was just a coincidence."

Why the confusion?

Tenenbaum and Griffiths believe that people have no problem detecting evidence of coincidences — they're not making up stories or seeing things that aren't there — they just tend to underestimate how much proof it takes to accept a theory. "The people of London were not at fault in recognizing that the rockets exhibited some evidence of clustering," they say, "but this evidence was certainly not sufficient to justify the conclusion that poorer parts of the city were being targeted."

DREAM WORLDS

R ita Dwyer developed rocket fuels for a leading aerospace lab back in the early days of the U.S. space program. "At the time, we didn't know about staging rocket engines, so we simply tried making more powerful fuels," she says. On April 23, 1959, the unthinkable happened: the highly sensitive propellants exploded, setting the research chemist and her lab on fire.

"I was burning to death," she says. "My safety glasses melted . . . and glass flew at my face and body. I tried dropping to the ground thinking I could roll and put out the fire, but the flames and debris surrounded me." Rita screamed for help, but no one answered. It looked like this might be the end. As the young woman slipped from consciousness, she whispered, "Dear God, ready or not, here I come." At that moment, a familiar voice called her name from the doorway.

Rita awoke in the arms of a technician, whom she assumed had rescued her. Weeks later she learned that the real hero was Ed Butler, a good friend and fellow chemist. Ed didn't feel much like a hero. In fact, he felt guilty — guilty because he never told Rita about a dream he'd had repeatedly for several weeks before the accident.

"In his dream he'd be sitting in his office lab working in his shirt sleeves without protection," says Rita. "He'd hear an explosion and go to the doors between the lab spaces and hear me screaming. Then he would call my name and go in to get me. He'd grab me by the one foot that wasn't burning, pull me into the safety shower, put out the flames, and then go to the red phone [a hotline for help]. When he got to the red phone, he'd wake up." Not this time. When Ed picked up the phone, someone answered his call, and he immediately realized this wasn't a dream. His nightmare had unfolded in real life.

No one knows why Ed had this "precognitive dream" — a dream that seems to foretell a future event. But the dream rehearsals clearly gave him the courage to rescue his coworker. "He didn't even think about what he was doing," says Rita. "He just followed the dream. . . . It really spooked both of us. Neither of us was superstitious or believed in dreams — we were straight scientists."

Today Rita believes in the therapeutic power of dreams to provide meaningful insights into people's waking lives and guide them through the rough spots. "All dreams bring information," says Rita, whose dreams helped her cope with the emotional and physical scars she suffered after the explosion. "Some are pat-on-the-back dreams that empower us, and others are kick-in-the-pants dreams that tell us when we're not doing what we should be doing. When a dream repeats itself, it wants us to pay attention." Ultimately, she says, only the dreamer knows the meaning of a dream.

ENCHANTING ENIGMAS

Dreams — whimsical or worrisome — have fascinated people through the ages. Ancient Mesopotamians believed good dreams hailed from the gods, and bad dreams derived from demons. To rid themselves of potential harm, people shared their unpleasant dreams with objects instead of other people. In one ritual, the dreamer tells his bad dream to a lump of clay that he's rubbed over his body and throws the clay into water so it will melt away future troubles.

One of the first to suggest that dreams originated with the dreamer and not the gods was the Greek philosopher Aristotle, who lived from 384 BCE to 322 BCE. "Animals were also observed to dream . . . and the

Panama's Cuna Indians deeply respect dreams and believe them to be prophetic. Here, a Cuna *nele*, or medicine man, sits with wooden *nuchu* figures. It's believed that the spirits of these figures travel with him in his dreams.

© Robert L. Van de Castle, *from* Our Dreaming Mind

gods would never send dreams to such lowly creatures [he reasoned]," says Dr. Robert Van de Castle in his book, *Our Dreaming Mind*. Aristotle also believed dreams could reveal the body's state of wellness and inspire people's waking behavior.

Modern theories about dreams began around the early 1900s, with Sigmund Freud's distinction between the conscious and unconscious mind. Freud believed dreams served as an outlet for people's repressed fears and desires and that talking about them would bring relief, primarily by revealing hidden thoughts and feelings to the conscious mind. Not long after, Carl Jung introduced the concept of the "collective unconscious" — a part of our unconscious he believed contained universal experiences and dream symbols understood by all peoples.

Dream research took a giant leap in the early 1950s when scientists at the University of Chicago discovered a stage of sleep characterized by rapid eye movement (REM) and brain activity similar to the waking state. During REM sleep, our eyes dart back and forth under the lids and our heart and breathing rates quicken. It's also the time we dream our most vivid dreams. To protect us from acting out these dreams, most of our muscles shut down during the REM phase — effectively paralyzing our bodies. Each night, we loop through about five ninety-minute sleep cycles distinguished by five stages.

The first four stages — generally referred to as non-REM sleep — shorten as the night progresses, while REM, the fifth stage of sleep, lengthens from about ten to thirty minutes. By the time we awake in the morning, we've usually had at least five dreams — adding up to more than 100,000 in a lifetime.

By the time we awake each morning, we've typically dreamed at least five times during the night. This translates to more than 100,000 dreams in a lifetime.

© *Shelley K. Frihauf*

What permeates our dreams? Many issues important to us during the day, says G. William Domhoff, a psychologist at the University of Santa Cruz in California who collaborates with colleagues to build, catalog, and maintain a collection of thousands of dreams reported by people of all ages. We dream about our hopes and fears, as well as future events and unfinished business, he says. A third of our dreams involve misfortunes — we lose keys or are unprepared for an exam. Children dream more about animals than teenagers and adults, he notes. Men and boys tend to dream about male characters and physical aggression; women and girls dream equally about both sexes and lean toward verbal aggression, such as insults.

While dreams vary by culture, a few universal themes thread our nights: falling; flying; losing teeth; being chased or attacked; and finding ourselves naked or inappropriately dressed in public. "Common dreams reflect how our brain works, how our social lives work," says dream expert Gayle Delaney. "We're all concerned about relationships with other people, our survival, and working out problems."

Today, many theories about dreams exist. Yet their role in our lives remains a mystery. Some believe we dream to psychologically adapt and adjust to life's issues. Many therapists, for example, view dreams as a reflection of a person's thoughts, emotions, and values, and work with dreams to treat illnesses such as anxiety and depression. Others hold an information-processing view of dreams. They believe dreams help us filter the day's events and consolidate our memories. Research shows that students who study and get a good night's rest score higher on tests than those who cram and take the test without sleeping. Still others see dreams as biological reactions. They believe dreams spring from random nerve signals that activate images from our memories and stir our emotions. Dreams, they say, are the brain's way of making sense of what's happening by creating stories.

Ultimately, the answer may lie in a dream theory that combines ideas from neurobiology and psychology, says Glen Gabbard of Baylor College of Medicine in Houston. "To have a truly comprehensive

The dreaming brain

Neuroimaging studies have shown which areas of the brain are most active and least active when a person is dreaming, providing some explanation for the characteristics of dreams.

A. LIMBIC SYSTEM

Emotions, memories

One of the most active areas during REM sleep is the limbic system, the seat of strong emotions, particularly fear and anxiety. This may explain dreams' strong emotional content.

Within the limbic system is the hippocampus, where episodic memory is stored. Research suggests sleep and dreaming are important for processing memories and certain types of learning.

B. MOTOR CORTEX

Motion

The motor cortex is active, contributing to dream content involving motion and perhaps also to learning certain skills.

C. PONS

Paralysis

Though the motor cortex is active, a switch inside the pons area of the brainstem prevents motor impulses from being transmitted to the body. This is why people are paralyzed during REM sleep, keeping them from acting out their dreams.

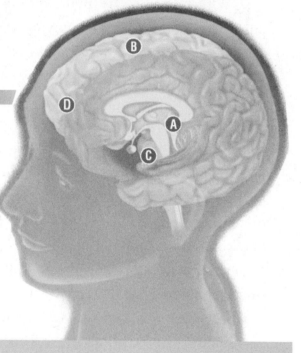

D. PREFRONTAL CORTEX

Irrationality

The most notable inactive area is the prefrontal cortex, the executive center associated with rational thought, decision making and intepretation of stimuli. This inactivity may explain the sometimes illogical, bizarre nature of dreams.

Amnesia

Short-term memory is located within the prefrontal cortex. The area's inactivity may explain why dreams often are hard to remember.

PET scans of sleeping brains

Pioneering studies of the sleeping brain using positron emission tomography, or PET, have been performed since the mid-1990s by Dr. Eric Nofzinger at the University of Pittsburgh. In these PET scans taken while the subject was in REM sleep, the bright areas outline the limbic system and show that it is very active, demonstrating that dreams are highly influenced by this emotional area of the brain.

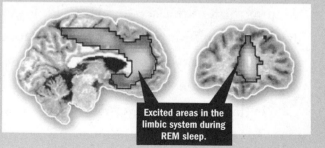

Excited areas in the limbic system during REM sleep.

The dreaming brain.

Illustration by: Byron Spice and Steve Thomas of the Pittsburgh Post–Gazette
Sources: University of Pittsburgh; Knight Ridder Tribune

understanding of dreams, you have to be bilingual. You have to speak the language of the mind and the language of the brain."

VIEW FROM A SLEEP LAB

Rosalind Cartwright, psychology chairman and founder of the sleep disorder research center at Rush University Medical Center in Chicago, has studied sleep and dreams for more than forty-five years. "What's the purpose of dreaming? That's like asking: What's the purpose of waking?" she says. "It's pretty variable." She believes dreams can serve many roles, depending on the degree to which people attend to them. "Some people just ignore them, can't remember them, and therefore deny they ever had any — which we know is wrong when we get them in the laboratory." Cartwright believes the overall purpose of dreaming is to regulate our moods and that one benefit of a good night's sleep is that our dreams tend to work through negative emotions.

Say a friend comments that "you're putting on a little weight." Maybe you blow off the remark during the day, but it registers at night. Your head hits the pillow and you eventually enter slow-wave sleep, a deep sleep that Cartwright says "seems to take whatever is emotionally important to you — whether you're conscious of it or not — and files it like a clip from previews of coming attractions." Next, REM sleep takes the information and connects it to previous memories with similar emotions. Perhaps a relative criticized you last summer at a family outing. That's when the dream story forms.

During REM sleep, the brain takes the various bits of information — past and present — and creates a narrative, says Cartwright. The story often looks bizarre because "you're laying one set of sensory images on top of other, older ones." You may think: *I had the craziest dream. Why did my friend look like my uncle Harry who I haven't seen in a while?* Well, it may be that Uncle Harry hurt your feelings the same way your friend's weight comment did — your dream just mixed the images, says Cartwright. "Finding the emotional link between images is the key to decoding the dream."

One reason we generally feel better in the morning, says Cartwright, is because we have four or five REM periods during the night, and each associated dream progressively works harder and reaches deeper into our memories to help us resolve issues. "If it's a mild affront, it's generally worked through and gone by morning so that you wake up in a good mood and go about your business," she says. But if the problems are too much to handle in one night, or if you've had no previous experience to relate it to — it's absolutely fresh — then (the dreams) can go on for many nights while you're building a new model of something that's important to you.

Dreams keep your self-concept — your idea of who you are — updated, believes Cartwright. "The things you dream about are those that are surprising or that throw you off course. The dream is saying, 'this has an impact on your idea of who you are.' It can help you adjust to a new facet of yourself that's being developed." Children, for instance, may have nightmares when they first begin to have angry feelings toward a parent, she says. "It's very scary for them." The important thing with nightmares is to remind the dreamer — young or old — that it's "an interesting story *they're telling themselves*," says Cartwright. "I always make the point that this is not something being done to them, it's something they've created. This gives the person control over the dream and allows them to [explore and] ask: *Why did I create that one?*"

Memory Makers

Dreams not only may provide insight, but some researchers believe they play a role in learning and memory. In a study conducted by Dr. Robert Stickgold and his colleagues at Harvard Medical School, people trained to play the computer game Tetris during the day began dreaming about falling pieces of the game at night — evidence, they say, that dreams help reinforce and integrate new information.

Rats also put their "dreams" to work, discovered Matthew Wilson, a professor of brain and cognitive sciences at MIT. Wilson led a study examining the brain activity of lab rats as they ran a maze and then again as they slept. He found that while the rats were sleeping, they replayed their maze-running experiences in both the brain's memory and vision centers.

In fact, patterns of neural activity matched so closely, the scientists could identify the rats' location in the maze as they dreamed. "This work brings us closer to an understanding of the nature of animal dreams and gives us important clues as to the role of sleep in processing memories of our past experiences," says Wilson.

"The mind doesn't turn off during dreaming — it just changes

Professor Matthew Wilson of MIT, shown here with one of his subjects wearing a brain-wave sensor, has found that rats replay maze-running experiences of the day in their dreams. Studies such as these may help us understand the role sleep and dreams play in learning and memory.

© AP Wide World Photos

channels," says Cartwright. "When we're awake, there's more attention to the outside world and to interacting with other people. You have to pay attention to reality or you'll get run over by a truck. But when we close our eyes to sleep, the brain doesn't need to be processing outside information . . . it doesn't need to communicate with anybody but itself."

Risa Nye's brain — and body — seemed to be trying to communicate with her for years. "The dreams were almost always the same," she writes in the *San Francisco Chronicle*. "My teeth were loose or falling out, or I had a huge wad of chewing gum in my mouth that I was unable to remove." Eventually, the forty-eight-year-old woman's back molars loosened and wiggled. Turns out, a benign cyst had been growing undetected in her mouth for most of her life. By the time it was discovered, the cyst had swollen to the size of a "ping-pong ball," she says. Almost immediately after the mass was removed, Risa's dental dreams stopped.

"This isn't the only case of its kind," says Cartwright, referring to what's known as a prodromal dream — a dream that signals illness before a person experiences symptoms. "There are so many incidents that people ask me: 'How do you explain that?' And I say, I don't know — yet. We're working on it."

⩗ MIND TINGLER

DREAM CATCHING

Want to remember your dreams? A good way to catch one is to wait until the weekend when you don't have to wake to an alarm clock, says sleep specialist Rosalind Cartwright. "Since the end of the night is very heavily REM time, you're more likely to wake spontaneously from a [vivid] REM dream."

The trick of remembering is to not move a muscle when you wake, she says. "Don't open your eyes and stay absolutely still. Since REM is the time you're without muscle tone, you want to keep that physiology going." It's also important to keep your eyes closed so you can keep the dream from fading and rehearse the last images in your mind. Next, give the dream a title, such as: *The ghost in the closet.*

"Once you give it a title, you can open your eyes and write,* because that will give you the key clue to the plot of the dream," says Cartwright. Write it exactly as you remember—even if it sounds a little crazy and jumps around. "You can do whatever you'd like with it afterward, but keep the raw data pure." It also helps to note any feelings the dream generated, says Rita Dwyer, past president of the International Association for the Study of Dreams.

In time, as you review your dreams, you'll see repeat images, words, and phrases, says Cartwright, and you'll begin to learn your own dream language.

*Be sure to have a pen, some paper, and/or a recorder near your bed before you go to sleep.

PURPLE NUMBERS
AND
POINTY CHICKENS

arol Crane "feels" music.

Guitars gently brush her ankle. Violins blow a soft breeze on her face. The trombone, on the other hand, pecks and pounds at the back of her neck. "I love to go to the symphony," says the pediatric neuropsychologist, "but when I come out I feel drained. It can be overwhelming."

Sean Day sees colors when he hears music, tastes food, or smells odors. If a saxophone's playing, neon purple appears. When the English professor bites into a steak, he sees dark blue. Every now and then, Sean puts together menus simply to watch the colors they'll create. "One of my favorites is a dinner entrée called 'chicken a la mode,' made with chicken, vanilla ice cream, and orange sauce — all of which appear to him as various shades of sky blue. It actually tastes pretty good," he says.

Carol and Sean have synesthesia, an unusual sensory condition characterized by the coupling of two or more senses. The name synesthesia rhymes with anesthesia and derives from the Latin *syn*, for together, and the Greek *aesthesis*, meaning sensation. Various forms of the condition exist — ranging from the pairing of numbers and letters to colors, to the rarer union of words and tastes. One man who tastes food whenever he hears words or verbalizes text (even in his dreams) says he has a "toffee-flavored nephew" and lives in a house tasting "of mashed potato," that's located in a "fruit gum town."

Estimates vary widely, but research led by Dr. Julia Simner, a neuropsychologist at the University of Edinburgh, recently found that as many as one in twenty-three people experience some type of synesthesia, which frequently runs in families. Carol's son and one of her sisters and nieces share the condition. About one-half of all "synesthetes," including Carol and Sean, experience several forms. In addition to feeling music, Carol experiences "time-shape" synesthesia, where the months of the year are represented visually on a Ferris wheel. "July is always on top and December is at the bottom," she says. "And I'm in the Ferris wheel car moving around through the year."

Some synesthetes, such as Sean Day, experience sensations such as colors and shapes outside their bodies. When Sean eats food, his colors appear at about arm's length, "a little higher than eye level and slightly to the left." His musical colors usually appear about halfway between his body and the source of the music, whether that's two feet away or fifty.

© AP Wide World Photos

In 1880, Sir Francis Galton published a report about the phenomenon, and while scientists showed a brief flurry of interest, many dismissed it until recently. Some saw it as a product of a vivid imagination, a cry for attention, or drug use. Drugs aren't totally implausible, says neurologist Dr. Richard Cytowic, who "accidentally rediscovered" the condition in 1980 when a dinner host commented that the meal wasn't ready because there "weren't enough points on the chicken." Several drugs can cause temporary synesthesia-like effects, he says, "but [synesthetes] experience this all the time, naturally throughout their whole life. As children, they're shocked to discover that the rest of the world's not like them."

No single diagnostic test exists for the various forms of synesthesia. However, Dr. Cytowic has identified general clinical characteristics of the condition, which include:

Involuntary and automatic: "It happens to you, as opposed to you doing anything special" to produce it, he says. Carol recognized her blended senses at about age four. Growing up, she'd ask people questions such as, "What color is your three?" and they'd look at her confused. Until recently, when she realized not everyone had her skill, Carol thought it was something she chose to do for enjoyment. "It never occurred to me that I had no choice in the matter," she says.

Consistent and generic: "Once established in childhood, synesthetic associations remain stable throughout life," says Dr. Cytowic. If A is blue in your alphabet, then it's always blue. If New York tastes like chocolate cake, then it always tastes like chocolate cake. Synesthesia also is generic in that the experiences are not complex, he says. "Where I might say listening to Beethoven makes me see sheep gamboling through a meadow . . . synesthetes would say I see zigzags, grids, or circles moving off to the right. Perceptually, it's very elementary."

Memorable: The sensations that accompany a particular word, shape, or piece of music generally make it easier for synesthetes to remember them. For example, some use the colors they see to recall people's names or phone numbers or to identify keys on the piano. At times, however, the condition can complicate matters. Some synesthetes find it frustrating, for instance, when their colored numbers or letters don't match those of the outside world. "If I park my car in a garage, and the number of the floor is [painted] in the wrong color," says Carol, "I have to make a conscious effort to remember one [color] or the other."

Despite such hurdles — and a few unpleasant associations — synesthesia is usually highly pleasurable for people, says Dr. Cytowic. Many integrate their experiences into creative pursuits, such as art, writing, and music. "On the other hand, mismatched perceptions can be like fingernails on the blackboard."

SENSORY PUZZLER

What causes synesthesia?

No one knows for sure, but researchers around the world are working to find out. They include Dr. Vilayanur Ramachandran, director of the Center for the Brain and Cognition at the University of California at San Diego, and Edward Hubbard, Ph.D., a postdoctoral fellow at INSERM in Orsay, France, who have worked together to understand what happens in the brain to cause synesthesia.

"We began with an embedded figures test" — also known as the

"pop-out" visual perception test — "to check for synesthesia in people who see numbers in color," explains Hubbard. "The basic logic behind this experiment is that if people who say they're seeing colors really are seeing colors, then you'd expect these colors to help them on certain tasks. So we created a display full of black 5s and embedded a triangle pattern of black 2s within it. If you or I were presented with this display, it would be very hard to find the triangle. But if somebody's really seeing colors — let's say they see red when they look at 5s and green when they look at 2s — then they should see a green triangle on a red background. And, in fact, that's what they saw — the green triangle jumped [or popped] out at them."

After validating their results by testing and retesting subjects over time, Ramachandran and Hubbard studied the brain's organization for answers. "We looked at various atlases of how the brain deals with color and recognizes letters and numbers," says Hubbard. Turns out, the area of the brain that initially processes color information sits right next to the area of the brain where visual number and letter shapes are represented.

Could this be a coincidence? The scientists didn't think so.

They suspected a cross-linking — physically or chemically — between the color and number-shape areas of the brain. Now the questions was, how might this happen?

"We've known almost since the beginning of synesthesia research that it runs in families," says Hubbard, "so we said maybe there's some sort of genetic factor causing these areas to be connected in some way or to be cross-wired." It could be that a gene — or set of genes — creates connections in the brain between regions normally separated.

Or it may be a type of short-circuit between neighboring brain regions, says Hubbard. "We know from numerous studies on how the brain develops that early in life there are lots of connections between brain regions." Normally, these connections are refined and pruned away as the brain matures. But there could be a genetic difference in how the pruning process unfolds in people with synesthesia, leaving them with extra connections, he says.

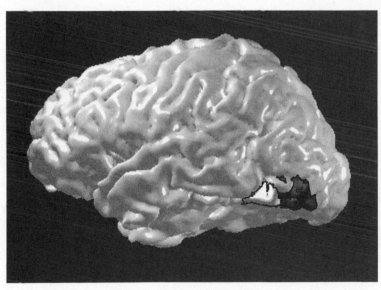

Researchers have found that the area of the brain that initially processes color information sits near a region of the brain where visual number and letter shapes are represented. They suspect that the two areas, shaded in the image at right, cross-link in people who see numbers and letters in color.

© *Imprint Academic, used with the permission of the* Journal of the Consciousness Studies

Such reasoning led Ramachandran and Hubbard to develop a "cross-activation" model of synesthesia — one of at least three major theories on how the condition might occur. "Essentially, the idea is that brain regions which normally become segregated in non-synesthetes remain more strongly connected in synesthetes, leading one region to 'cross activate' the other," explains Hubbard. For example, when activity in the number-recognizing area of the brain cross-activates the color region, people see colors when they view numbers.

Brain imaging experiments lend support to the scientists' cross-activation theory. "On presenting black and white numbers to synesthetes, brain activation arose not only in the number area — as it would in normal subjects — but also in the color area," they report.

CREATIVE CONNECTIONS

Colors and numbers aren't the only regions in the brain that appear to cross-talk. Researchers have identified other adjacent areas that could explain some of the rarer types of synesthesia. A man who tastes shapes may cross-activate the taste-processing regions of his brain with the nearby somatosensory cortex, which handles touch sensations, they say. A woman for whom letters of the alphabet, days of the week, and months of the year all have personalities — "February is an introvert, May is soft-spoken, and August is a boy among girls" — may cross-activate the part of the brain that addresses ordinal sequences (123, ABC, etc.) with a neighboring region that assigns personalities to people, according to Simner and Hubbard.

"We started out very narrowly—looking at colors, letters, and numbers—and tried to see how many of these unusual extra-experiences we could account for using the same brain mechanism," says Hubbard, referring to his work with Ramachandran. The possibilities they found made them wonder: Could similar connections exist between other areas of the brain — say, those responsible for concepts and ideas? Maybe synesthesia could help explain creativity, given that it's thought to be more prevalent among poets, artists, and novelists.

One skill many creative people share is a knack for metaphor, note the researchers. Metaphors are figures of speech that use the imagination to directly link two seemingly unrelated subjects, as in "dark secret," "warm reception," and "bittersweet memories." Ramachandran says it's possible artistic people have extra connections between brain regions that allow them to associate concepts more easily than others. (This same process could occur with numbers and other high-level ideas.)

Such gifts aren't limited to a select group — we're all synesthetes to some degree, say the scientists. To prove it, they ask people to look at two shapes: one that resembles a curvy amoeba and the other that looks like a jagged piece of glass. In "Martian" language, one of these shapes is a "kiki" and the other a "bouba." Which one do you think is the kiki?

If you answered the jagged-glass shape, then you're in sync with 98 percent of people tested, they say. Why a jagged kiki? Probably because the sound *kiki* is sharp like the pointed edges of the visual image. "What you're seeing is a deep similarity in terms of jaggedness, despite the fact that one is visual and the other is auditory," says

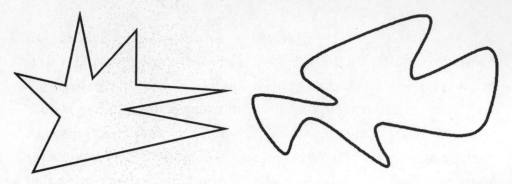

Which shape do you think is the "kiki" and which do you think is the "bouba"? Most people say the jagged shape is the kiki because it's sharp-sounding like the image.

© Edward Hubbard, Ph. D.

Hubbard. "We think what's happening with the metaphor is exactly the same sort of thing — seeing this deep similarity."

By exploring the mysteries of synesthesia, researchers and others hope to gain further insights into how the brain combines information from the different senses and how it may transform sensory messages into more abstract thoughts.

For a scientist, the fun and excitement begin with "I don't know," says Hubbard. "That's what's happening with synesthesia research. We know a lot about how the brain works to see colors and how it deals with numbers, and so on. But, in fact, there are a lot more questions than answers."

MIND TINGLER

SYNESTHESIA Q&A

Q. What's the most common type of synesthesia?
A. Research suggests "colored days" is the most common form. Synesthesia involving "colored letters and numbers" (A elicits red, B elicits blue, and so on) is the most frequently studied.

Q. How many types of synesthesia exist?
A. No one knows for sure, but the number is likely to be large. In addition to the sensory pairings across the five senses — vision, hearing, touch, taste, and smell — synesthesia exists within a single sense, such as seeing colors from viewing numbers. There also may be some types of synesthesia that do not involve the senses at all.

Q. Do synesthetes agree on what color letters should be?
A. Yes and no. Two synesthetes will often argue about the color of letters. But when researchers look at a very large sample of synesthetes, significant preferences emerge. For instance, A is often red, B is often blue, S is often yellow, and so on. Shared preferences also can be found in other types of synesthesia. For example, people who experience colors with music tend to agree that high notes are lighter in color than low notes.

Q. Can you be a synesthete in several languages?
A. Yes. One woman who is trilingual experiences colors for English, Spanish, and French words.

Q. Can synesthesia occur for touch and other body sensations?

A. Yes. For instance, a person may have different shapes or colors triggered by pain or touch. One synesthete experienced different shapes for different types of headaches and focused on the shape to try to control the pain.

Q. Are the brains of synesthetes different?

A. Most likely—but their brains are not damaged in any way. Most theories of synesthesia point to "cross-talk" between areas of the brain that might not otherwise communicate.

Q. Can synesthesia ever be lost?

A. Some people say they've experienced synesthesia, but have grown out of it. This leads to the possibility that synesthesia may be more common among preschoolers than adults. Synesthesia also could potentially be lost following drug use or brain injury.

Source: Synesthesia FAQ developed by Julia Simner, Ph.D., at the University of Edinburgh in the United Kingdom, with multilanguage answers provided by Edward Hubbard, Ph.D.

ARTISTIC TOUCH

I sometimes wonder if the hand is not more sensitive to the beauties of sculpture than the eye. I should think the wonderful rhythmical flow of lines and curves could be more subtly felt than seen.

— Helen Keller, deaf and blind author and activist

Esref Armagan smoothes his fingers over the bronze statue of Hans Christian Andersen in New York's Central Park. His thick hands survey the breadth of the chest, the span of the arms, and the placement of each finger. When he's absorbed enough of the figure's form, Esref turns to the sculpture of a duck nearby, deftly exploring its sleek lines.

The Turkish artist sketches an image of the scene, along with a picture of a helicopter he hears flying overhead. His drawings mirror the objects around him, but he welcomes affirmation from others.

Esref is blind in both eyes, and indications are he has been since birth. He's never seen a duck or a helicopter. He's never witnessed butterflies in flight, fish darting in the ocean, or a field of wildflowers

winding up a mountainside. Yet he can draw them in detail from any angle. "I do not know if the things I make are beautiful," he says. "I only know the reactions of others."

Esref Armagan sketches the sculpture of a duck in New York's Central Park. The blind artist draws on a special clipboard with a rubberized surface that allows him to create images with his right hand, which leave impressions for his left hand to follow.

© David E. Simpson, Panacea Pictures
Photo by Slawomir Grünberg

BEGINNER'S STROKES

Born in 1953 to an impoverished family living in Istanbul, Esref's life as an artist began at about six years old. "In those days, I would draw with a nail and cardboard," he says. Isolated from his peers and family, Esref passed the time sketching shapes on cardboard boxes his father brought home from work, says his friend and manager, Joan Eroncel. Eventually, he drew objects around him and learned how to paint and add colors, shading, shadows, and perspective to his work. Perspective is an advanced technique artists use to create the illusion of a three-dimensional image on a flat surface.

Esref Armagan has never seen fish swimming in the ocean, but he can conceptualize and paint them from any angle.

© Zafer Kizilkaya, Images and Stories

How did he learn? In part, by asking questions. "What color is the sky?" "What color are the clouds?" "What are their shapes?" Esref mistakenly thought blue objects had blue shadows and yellow objects had yellow shadows until someone explained how shadows worked. Even the concept of color had to be described to him.

Some of Esref's art is rooted on what he's been taught by friends and acquaintances, says John M. Kennedy, a psychologist at the University of Toronto who has studied artistic development and ability in the blind for more than thirty years. "But a lot of what he's doing is probably based on his own direct experience with objects. As far as I can tell, nobody's told him what you do with a line: that a line can stand for the edge of a surface; that a line can stand for a corner; that a line can stand for the edge of a roof. These are things that seem to come naturally to him."

Esref draws on a special clipboard with a rubberized surface called a Sewell raised-line drawing kit. The tool enables him to create lines and images on paper with his right hand that leave impressions for his left hand to feel and follow as a guide. Where sighted people use vision to draw, the blind artist uses touch to conceptualize the "big picture" and keep track of items on the page.

Esref composes each painting in his mind before applying fast-drying acrylic paints with his fingers. He works with seven tubes of color — white, black, yellow, brown, red, blue, and green — each carefully lined in front of him in a sequence he's memorized.

Kennedy's years of research indicate that the ability to draw in

At right, John M. Kennedy, a psychologist at the University of Toronto, tests Esref Armagan's artistic skills. Kennedy believes blind and sighted people develop the ability to draw in much the same way.

© David E. Simpson, Panacea Pictures.
Photo by Slawomir Grünberg

blind and sighted people develops much the same way. A blind child who draws a lot "often will draw very similarly to a sighted child of the same age," he says. "However, it's very rare to find a blind child who has been encouraged to draw a lot." Esref's lifelong history as an artist allowed Kennedy to test some of his theories about art and the abilities of the blind.

In one instance, Kennedy placed a wooden cube, cone, and ball in front of Esref and asked him to draw it from his point of view as well as from the point of view of someone sitting to his left and to his right. Esref placed his hands over the objects and thought for a few moments. "He held his hands in front of his face, as if they were touching a picture surface." Then he started to draw, and "succeeded in imagining each of the vantage points that those people would have," says Kennedy. By accurately drawing the scenes, Esref became the first blind person the Canadian researcher had met to demonstrate a mastery of three-point perspective — creating images that realistically represent the height, width, and depth of objects from various viewpoints. "Sighted people like to say that they are visualizing things," says Kennedy. "A good word for what Esref is doing is spacializing. He does that in [his mind] and then works out the implications on the page."

Esref's exceptional talents have captured the attention of the art world, with museums around the globe from Chicago to Shanghai displaying his work. At a New York Turkish Consulate exhibit, one admirer beamed: "Where he creates depth and perspective in something like the mountains and waterfalls . . . it's absolutely extraordinary."

Esref Armagan paints with the depth and perspective of a sighted person.

© Zafer Kizikaya, Images and Stories

PROBING THE BRAIN

Art enthusiasts aren't the only people in awe of Esref's talents. Neuro-scientists value the opportunity to study the brain's plasticity — how well it changes and adapts in response to new information and expe-riences. How, they ask, can a blind man draw and paint as if he could see? How does his brain form mental images of objects — gained

103

primarily through touch — which he's able to illustrate in pictures sighted people understand and recognize?

To learn more about the inner workings of Esref's brain, Dr. Alvaro Pascual-Leone, professor of neurology at Harvard Medical School and director of the Berenson-Allen Center for Noninvasive Brain Stimulation at Beth Israel Deaconess Medical Center, invited the blind artist to Boston for testing in July 2004.

"For somebody to feel an object by hand and draw it [accurately], a few things have to happen," explains Pascual-Leone. "First, the person needs to be able to extract information about the object by touch." Then the brain must convert the information into a mental image of the object's shape. Finally, the person must be capable of depicting that mental image in a drawing, he says.

Esref is unique in that, as a blind person, he can both capture images in his mind through touch *and* translate these internal images into drawings as precisely as any sighted gifted artist. By having these two abilities, says Dr. Pascual-Leone, Esref offers an opportunity to explore three important questions:

  • Is his internal representation of objects fundamentally the same as a sighted person's?

  • What part or parts of the brain are working to generate the images he sees in his mind's eye?

  • And what areas of the brain translate the internal image into a drawing?

To find out, Pascual-Leone and his colleagues asked Esref to feel a series of objects — including a comb, coffee cup, hammer, toothbrush, and toy sailboat — for thirty seconds while he lay on his back in a functional magnetic resonance imaging (fMRI) machine. The machine measures blood flow in the brain and indicates the active regions during mental activity. Esref then had thirty seconds to draw the objects on a tablet resting on his belly.

Dr. Alvaro Pascual-Leone tests Esref's skills, as Dr. Elif Ozdemir helps translate instructions into Turkish.

© David E. Simpson, Panacea Pictures.
Photo by Slawomir Grünberg

The results?

"We found that he activates the visual shape parts of the brain, even though he's never seen," says Pascual-Leone. "He also activates the visual cortex — the part of the brain that would normally light up when you actually see an object [with your eyes]. This is the same pattern of activity that you'd find in a sighted person imagining an object. . . . The activity in his brain — what he imagines and then translates into a drawing — is exactly the same as a sighted person who's actually seeing an object."

For Dr. Pascual-Leone, who has been studying the blind and loss of sight for more than fifteen years, these results support his theory that the brain is organized by various "operators" that perform tasks based on the sensory information available.

"Imagine that you have a part of the brain that figures out the shape of things," he says. "You can figure out the shape of something by looking at it or feeling it. So this part of the brain waits for information: Is there visual information available about the shape? If there is, it will use that because it's better suited. But if there's no visual information available, it will ask the fingertips: Is there any tactile information? And if there is, it will use that instead. The same part of the brain figures out the shape of things — whether the information is visual or tactile."

BLINDFOLD STUDIES

Pascual-Leone finds further evidence of the brain's plasticity in his ongoing studies of sighted people who volunteer to be blindfolded for five days and learn skills such as reading Braille. Before the blindfolding, brain scans of volunteers show little activity in the visual areas when they engage in tasks involving touch. After five sightless days, however, the visual cortex lights up when volunteers take part in tactile activities such as reading Braille. The vision center, it appears, is processing touch information because it's not receiving any visual input from the eyes.

Two hours after researchers remove the blindfolds from volunteers, brain scans revert back to their previously sighted status. Pascual-Leone explains that with sensory data coming from the eyes, the visual cortex probably has less time to deal with tactile issues and masks the activities of the other senses. Our senses do not work in isolation, he says. "When we see something, we're not just seeing it — we're also hearing, smelling, and touching it with our minds — even if we're not *actually* hearing, smelling, or touching it. All this sensory information shapes what we see and how we see it."

Given this, scientists can help people compensate for deficits through their other senses. It's called sensory substitution, and while it's not new, researchers are taking it to greater heights. One developing technology now helps blind people "see" with their ears.

Pat Fletcher dreamed of becoming a veterinarian. As a child, she'd pull out her doctor's kit and practice on the family's twelve-pound Chihuahua. "Susie would tolerate my efforts to listen to her heart with my plastic stethoscope," says Pat. "But for some reason, she was not very happy with me when I tried to take her temperature. . . . I still carry a small scar on my right hand to remind me of that examination." The second of six children, Pat spent her teens in the Appalachian Mountains of Kentucky, where she hiked local trails and camped under the stars.

In August 1979, Pat graduated with honors from Cumberland College in Williamsburg, Kentucky. Armed with a bachelor's degree in biology and minors in chemistry and the ROTC (Reserve Officers' Training Corps), she prepared for veterinary school in Gainesville, Florida.

One week later, her life changed forever. A chemical explosion at the demolition plant where Pat worked perforated her right eye and sealed shut her left. "I remember looking out and seeing blue all around me," she says. "I knew it was flames, but I was surprised, because I didn't feel any pain. . . . I remember looking up and this guy named Alfred came out. He was bringing me a fire blanket, and that's the last thing I saw when he threw it over my head. "

For more than twenty years, Pat lived in darkness. Only in dreams did the images of her youth resurface. "I learned how to be a blind person," she says. "I learned to use a cane, worked with guide dogs, and eventually picked up my first computer. . . . I just knew [the computer] had to be a means out."

Was it ever. In 1998 — after teaching herself everything from setting up a computer to programming it — Pat stumbled upon something amazing. "I was looking for a software program to help me identify the colors of my clothing using the scanner, and I found it on a Web site that offered technology for the blind. So I downloaded the program and was a happy camper. Now I could pull out a T-shirt and tell whether it was blue or red."

Pat explored the site further. What was this talk about seeing with sound? "At first, it was over my head," she says. But the demonstration files intrigued her, so she launched one called *Bright wall with gate.*

"I had speakers on each side of the room," she explains. "So I looked to the left to make sure that the sound was working, and then I looked to the right. When I looked to the right, I saw what looked like a three-dimensional image crossing the room — something like a hologram. "At first, I thought, 'No way!' It startled me — I wasn't expecting this. It couldn't be real. Then I got up off my seat and actually walked along the length of it. It was as if I was walking right by a real gate. I walked up to the back part of the gate and almost wanted to stick out my hand and touch it, because I just knew there would be some blackberries there." Once Pat "saw" and "experienced" the gate, she knew this program was going to somehow create vision for her.

THE vOICe (OH I SEE!)

The technology transforming Pat's life is called The vOICe and was invented by a research physicist in the Netherlands named Peter Meijer. The vOICe converts video images it receives from a camera into highly complex sounds called soundscapes. Once the brain picks up these sound patterns — through speakers or headphones — it decodes the information into gray-scale visual images.

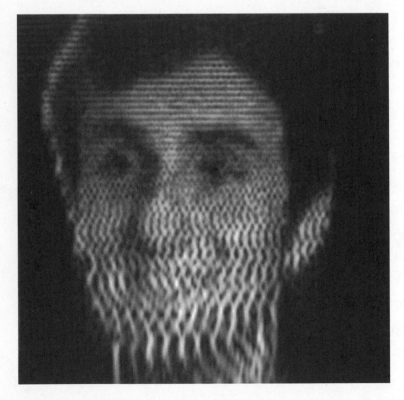

The vOICe technology converts images from a camera into sound patterns called soundscapes. Pictured is a visual computer reconstruction of one second of audible sound, as generated by the vOICe. "This proves that even complex, real-life images can be largely preserved in the image-to-sound mapping," says inventor Peter Meijer.

Courtesy of Peter Meijer

Meijer formulated the idea for The vOICe in 1983 while a student at Delft University of Technology. "I wanted to learn more about digital technology," he says, "preferably by designing something new that could benefit people." At the time, Meijer faced many hurdles — the first of which was to prove that images "could indeed be preserved in sound."

Today, the innovative scientist says his creation continues to evolve, but follows a few basic rules:

1. The vOICe captures a new image every second and turns it into sound. A person who stares at an object will repeatedly hear the same sounds.

2. Every image is scanned in stereo, from left to right. Objects on the left will be heard through the left ear; objects on the right will be heard through the right ear.

3. Volume indicates the brightness of an object: the louder the brighter. Silence represents black.

4. Pitch denotes elevation: The higher the pitch, the higher the object's position; the lower the pitch, the lower the object's position.

"All of this is sufficient to convey any black-and-white image in a second of sound, with a reasonable resolution of about four thousand pixels," says Meijer. "For example, if you have a bright diagonal line running from the bottom left to the upper right in your view, you hear something like *ooiieep, ooiieep, ooiieep*, as the image gets refreshed every second. A bright rectangle sounds much like a noise burst that starts and stops suddenly, a bit like *psjjjjt, psjjjjt."*

If multiple objects appear in your camera's view, you may hear them simultaneously, and this is where things can become complex, says Meijer. "Mentally disentangling the sound components of multiple items in a typical view — such as a view of your environment — is very difficult to master."

PIONEERING JOURNEY

Pat initially explored The vOICe program using a desktop computer, stereo headset, and a scanner. "At first, the soundscapes were confusing and just a bunch of blurry noise," she says. The flat, two-dimensional pictures of apples and other items on her scanner were more difficult for her mind to decipher than the three-dimensional gate she'd seen earlier.

But Pat practiced and persevered. Each day she placed pictures of objects on the scanner and compared them to their soundscapes. Still, she needed something more to help her connect the strange sounds with sight. That something turned out to be a multi-sensory approach involving touch.

"I put a cup on my scanner and took an image file of it for the program," she says. "Then I held the cup in my hand, put on my headphones, and listened." Concentrating carefully, Pat slowed down the program and used the arrow keys on her keyboard to move up and down the image, as well as side to side.

"Suddenly, I started connecting," she says. "I thought: *Here's the lip of the cup, and look, it has designs on it.* I had felt the designs before with my hands, but it never connected to me that there could be an image." Feeling the cup and hearing the soundscape helped Pat's brain understand what she was "seeing." "I realized that this was not just an image anymore—this was starting to make an image in my head that connected to what I remembered a cup would look like."

Pat's next major breakthrough came when she "let go of the desktop" and went mobile with The vOICe program. "My first setup included a small Web cam fastened on the bill of a baseball cap, large stereo headphones with a boom microphone, and a heavy computer notebook on my back," she says. "I ran the USB cable out the back of

Pat Fletcher wears video sunglasses with a small camera and ear buds attached to it, which help her "see with sound." The glasses connect to a laptop computer Pat carries in a backpack. The computer runs The vOICe software.

© Barbara Schweizer

115

the ball cap and down into a backpack. It was a wild snarl of wires . . . and the heat from the computer against my back was incredible."

Despite the bulky gear, Pat pressed on. "All I wanted was to see what things were," she says. "When you're blind, your world is limited by the objects immediately around you." Pat longed to reach beyond these artificial boundaries and expand her world. "I'll never forget looking down my hallway and seeing blinds hanging on the window," she says. Something so simple, yet I just couldn't believe it. I knew these things were here, but didn't relate them to my everyday world."

Today, Pat's mobile gear is lighter and more efficient: She wears "spyglasses" rigged with a tiny camera and microphone, a pair of headphones, and a backpack containing a lightweight laptop computer. "Now when I'm walking down the street toward you, it looks like I'm wearing a pair of sunglasses and listening to a Walkman," she says.

From a distance, Pat generally can tell if you're an adult or a child based on size. As she moves closer, her other senses kick in. "I can feel the thickness and height of the approaching form," she says. "My mind also will listen and determine the pattern of the step." Is the person wearing high heels? Then it's probably a woman. Pat can't distinguish facial expressions or note the color of your eyes. "But I can see you," she says. It's not the detailed vision you get from your eyes, but it is seeing."

Among the most treasured gifts Pat's newfound sight offers is an opportunity for her to rediscover nature's beauty. "We have a great big tree on our sidewalk, and I walked over to it and realized that the side of it had been split open," she says. "I could hear the wave of the roughness in the bark. It got to me . . . just the whole experience of being able to see a tree again."

When she visited Tucson, Arizona, and met Peter Meijer — the creator of The vOICe — for the first time, Pat saw cactus plants in the desert "with their arms tilted and bent up."

Then she looked out and noticed "lots and lots of points."

"What's that?" she asked Peter.

"You can see that?" he said. "You're looking at mountains."

"Mountains," she said — tears streaming down her face. "My mountains."

Pat Fletcher first met the creator of The vOICe software, Peter Meijer, in Tucson, Arizona, where she also had the opportunity to "see" many cactus plants in the desert.

Courtesy of Peter Meijer

MIND TINGLER

SENSES OUT OF SYNC

Imagine wearing a turtleneck year 'round to protect yourself from breezes brushing your skin or walking on tiptoes to avoid uncomfortable sensations at the bottom of your feet. Now imagine smelling every scent in a room simultaneously or hearing planes fly overhead as clearly as someone snapping his fingers beside you in class.

Children with Sensory Integration Dysfunction (SID) don't have to imagine these scenarios—many live with symptoms like these each day. Some receive too much information from their senses and become hypersensitive to touch, taste, smell, sound, and/or movement. Others receive too little information and crave stimulation from vigorous activities such as rocking, jumping, and spinning. These children may have reduced awareness of temperature or pain and behave like daredevils.

"Sensory integration is the organization of sensations for use," explains A. Jean Ayres, Ph.D., who first identified the condition in the 1960s. When the brain processes sensory input in a "well-organized or integrated manner," we can effectively interpret and respond to our environment, she says. When sensations are disorganized, "life can be like a rush-hour traffic jam," and responses are out of sync.

Each child experiences sensory integration difficulties differently, depending on the areas affected. Children who feel touch sensations too easily or intensely, for example, may be irritated—and distracted—by lotions, sock seams, and clothing tags. Their peers, on the other hand, may display poor coordination because they're not receiving appropriate input from their muscles and joints. As a result, they may distrust their bodies and avoid activities they can't completely control—just one way the condition can spill into a child's day-to-day life.

Fortunately, identifying symptoms early and providing children with a sensory workout in a safe environment can help minimize its social, emotional, and academic effects. Occupational therapists, for example, use "play" therapy to stimulate a child's various sensory systems and guide them into providing proper feedback.

No one has perfect sensory integration, explains Ayres. But those with well-integrated senses generally live happier, more productive lives.

BRAIN PHANTOMS: HAUNTING THE BODY

Sometimes it feels like someone's driving a knitting needle through my [right] big toe. The pain can be excruciating," says Tom Whittaker. Then he remembers: he doesn't have a big toe . . . or a right foot.

Whittaker — an avid sportsman and mountaineer born in Wales — lost his lower right leg in 1979 when a car crashed head-on into his Volkswagon bus.

Up until then, the thirty-one-year-old had led a life of adventure, "making the first ascent of a thousand-foot frozen waterfall in the Canadian Rockies, climbing alone to the summit of Mount McKinley, Alaska, and scaling the three-thousand-foot nose of El Capitan in Yosemite Valley, California."

Determined to preserve what he could of his limbs, Whittaker refused pain medicine after the accident until he could talk with the surgeon and explain that his life and livelihood depended on physical activity. The strategy paid off. Instead of losing both lower legs, Whittaker awoke from surgery with his left leg intact. The doctor had performed a special amputation — called a Symes amputation — which preserved his heel and allowed the foot to bear weight. "That gives

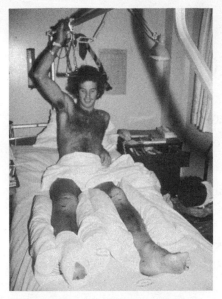

After a car accident in 1979, Tom Whittaker lost his lower right leg and part of his left foot. This photo was taken in the hospital before his surgery.

© Tom Whittaker Collection

me a huge advantage in terms of mobility," he says.

After months of physical and psychological recovery, Whittaker gradually returned to his active life — climbing, kayaking, and mountaineering — with renewed passion.

Almost twenty years later, on May 27, 1998, he made history by becoming the first disabled man to summit Mount Everest. "When you take a 'you'll never walk again' prognosis all the way to the roof of the world," he says, "you've covered a lot of terrain."

Tom Whittaker crosses a crevasse in Khumbu Icefall. An avid sportsman, Whittaker continued mountaineering despite being an amputee.

© Tom Whittaker Collection

EERIE SENSATIONS

Tom Whittaker may have been the first amputee to climb to the top of Mount Everest, but he's not the first to feel the vivid presence of a missing part of his body. Many people continue to be keenly aware of and experience "phantom" sensations in limbs they've lost. Some say their missing hands wave "hello" and their amputated arms swing as they walk. Others report feeling rings on lost fingers or having missing limbs that become hot, cold, itchy, and/or stuck in awkward positions.

"Just after the amputation, the phantom usually feels as though it is the same size and shape as the amputated portion of the limb," writes Richard A. Sherman, a researcher who has surveyed thousands of military amputees about their experiences. "Most people feel that they can move and control it as well as they could control the limb itself. The sensations are so real and normal that many young, traumatic, lower-limb amputees frequently try to get up and walk away a day or so after their amputations."

Phantoms can be helpful — they often animate an artificial limb by keeping "alive" the memory of an arm or leg. However, most amputees also report pain and discomfort from their lost limbs. This phantom pain can be agonizing and feels as real as any other, explains Dr. Jonathan Cole, a neurophysiologist, researcher and author from England. "It's been described as 'burning,' 'aching,' 'tightening,' 'clenching,' 'fingernails against a blackboard,' 'red hot coals,' and a 'hand being crushed in a vise.'"

Whittaker — whose missing right big toe sometimes feels like it's being pierced by a knitting needle — says the pain lasts seconds, "but the intensity is such that it makes my nostrils flare." He says the pain occurred more frequently soon after his amputation, but that it still happens occasionally — "usually while I'm sitting around in the evening or recreating with friends. We'll be at a barbecue and all of a sudden I'll start jumping around." What's frustrating is not being able to address the issue, he says. "How do you scratch it or grab it or do anything to it if it's not there?"

Tom Whittaker rests after summiting Mount Aconcagua in January 2001. Whittaker, who sometimes suffers phantom limb pain, was the first disabled man to summit Mount Everest in May 1998.

© Tom Whittaker Collection

People born without arms and legs also experience phantom sensations — though not pain — which suggests that the perception of our limbs is hardwired in our brains, says Dr. Cole. Research indicates that "the body we perceive in large part is built into our brain — it's not entirely learned," says psychologist Ronald Melzack. "In fact, you don't need the body to feel the body."

Our brain contains a sensory "map" of the various parts of our body: the knee, the hand, the shoulders. This map — discovered and charted by Canadian brain surgeon Wilder Penfield in the mid-1900s — is located in the primary somatosensory cortex, a long strip of tissue stretched between our ears where nerve cells process touch, temperature, and pain signals. When a person loses a limb, the sensory region in the brain corresponding to that body part remains intact waiting for messages from the touch receptors. Some scientists believe that when no messages come in, restless nerve cells may seek new connections and change the brain's sensory map.

Dr. Vilayanur Ramachandran tells the story of how one man's brain adjusted to the loss of a limb.

"I once had a patient whose arm had been amputated above the left elbow. He sat in my office blindfolded while I gently touched different areas of his body and asked him to say where I was touching him. All went as expected until I touched his left cheek, at which point he exclaimed, 'Oh my God, you're touching my left thumb,' his missing phantom thumb, in other words. He seemed as surprised as I was. Touching his upper lip produced sensation in his phantom index finger, and touching his lower jaw provoked sensations in his phantom little finger. There was a complete, systematic map of the missing phantom hand draped on his face.

How could this be? Dr. Ramachandran looked to the brain's sensory map for answers.

As it happens, the sensory center representing the face sits next to the area associated with the hand. When the hand region stopped

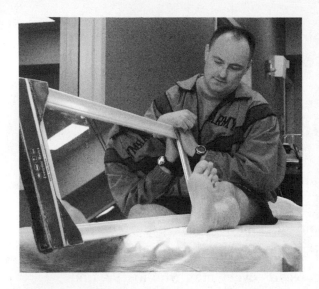 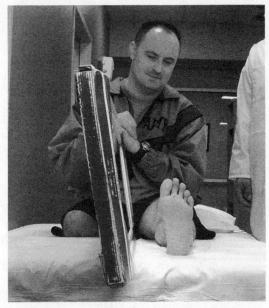

While serving in Iraq, Army Sergeant Nicholas Paupore lost his right leg below the knee In an explosion. Soon after, he began feeling taser-like phantoms in his missing limb. When pain medications didn't help, he volunteered for clinical trials of mirror therapy that were modeled after Dr. Vilayanur Ramachandran's ground-breaking studies. The results "astounded" U.S. Navy Commander Jack Tsao, who coordinated the trials at Walter Reed Army Medical Center in Virginia. All eighteen participants experienced relief, including Paupore, who says he's now nearly pain-free. Above, Paupore demonstrates how he uses the mirror to "see" and "flex" his missing leg, so that his brain receives all the information it needs to keep the phantom limb from hurting.

MC3 Jeff Hopkins, Courtesy of the United States Navy

receiving touch signals, it became "hungry for sensory input," theorized Dr. Ramachandran. Soon, he says, nerve cells from the face area crossed into the hand region of the brain, causing the two to overlap. "Signals from the face [were] then misinterpreted by higher centers in the brain as arising from the missing hand," he explains. Dr. Ramachandran later verified his hypothesis using brain-imaging, which showed that when the patient's face was touched, activity occurred in both the face and hand regions of the brain. "This is very different

127

from what is seen in a normal brain, where touching the face activates only the facial region of the cortex," he says.

GHOSTS OF THE PAST

Phantom limbs — and pain — have probably always existed, but few people addressed the issue until shortly after the Civil War, when Dr. Silas Weir Mitchell described and documented the experiences of soldiers and other amputees. In 1872, he wrote in his book, *Injuries of Nerves and Their Consequences*: "Nearly every man who loses a limb carries about with him a constant or inconstant phantom of the missing member, a sensory ghost of that much of himself, and sometimes a most inconvenient presence, faintly felt at times, but ready to be called up to his perception by a blow, a touch, or a change of wind."

Doctors once thought phantom limb pain and sensations lived in their patient's imaginations — one reason people seldom discussed them. Eventually, the focus switched to the site of the amputation, where nerves in a patient's stump might be injured. "Damage to the nerve endings is often important," says Dr. Cole. A person may have a neuroma — an abnormal collection of nerve cells or tumor at the site — which can be painful. Surgeons often try to cut out neuromas, says Dr. Cole. "But that only works for a short time. Then the pain can and does come back." In fact, once a phantom limb becomes painful, "it's rarely improved by current medical treatments," says Dr. Cole. Good news is on the horizon, however, as researchers turn their attention to the brain — "the center of pain processing."

Dr. Ramachandran demonstrated that the brain can play tricks on a person with a lost limb by cross-wiring sensory connections. He wondered: Could the reverse be true? Can a person fool his brain into easing phantom limb pain?

The chance to find out presented itself when a man came to him with an agonizingly painful phantom hand that was frozen in a tight fist he couldn't unclench no matter how hard he tried. Using a cardboard box with a mirror propped sideways inside it, Dr. Ramachandran asked the man to take his good arm and mimic the position of his painful phantom. He then directed the man to look at the mirror and slowly uncurl his hand, pretending it was his phantom. The idea was to give the brain visual feedback and trick it into believing it was following the man's instructions to relax the missing hand.

Sure enough, the man felt relief as he watched his hand in the mirror. "The movements have all come back," he told the doctor. Once the mirror was removed, however, the pain returned. Dr. Ramachandran believes this may have happened because the man's arm and hand "learned" to be paralyzed through years of disuse before his amputation and needed to be unlearned. As the man practiced with the mirror box, his condition improved.

MIND GAMES

Dr. Ramachandran's pioneering work suggests that phantom limb pain may develop from both a loss of sensory signals to the brain as well as a lack of motor feedback — information about the movements of the missing limb. The phantom can't tell the brain what it's doing—clenching or unclenching—if it doesn't exist.

Mirror-box research also set the stage for related studies aimed at using visual tricks to fool the brain. One study found that patients could ease phantom limb pain by simply imagining that their arms were moving in sync with an arm projected on a screen.

NASA's Robonaut provided a virtual reality model for Dr. Jonathan Cole's research on brain phantoms.

Courtesy of NASA

Taking the concept one step further, Dr. Cole and a team of scientists are modeling their research after a virtual reality system at NASA's Johnson Space Center in Houston, Texas. "NASA had this wonderful robot (called Robonaut) with arms which move like people's arms," Dr. Cole told the Wellcome Trust, a London-based medical research charity. "They give you a virtual reality headset, and fit your arms and hands into gloves with infrared sensors. Looking down, instead of your own arms, you see the robot's arms via cameras mounted in the robot's head. When you move your arms, the robot arms move in exactly the same way, only more slowly. Within a minute you feel completely embodied in the robot: what we see and move we become."

It's called telepresence — in this case using virtual reality to feel "at one" with the robot — and Dr. Cole's research team is testing to see if a similar experience would ease phantom limb pain. They've developed a virtual arm, which can be projected on a screen or in virtual reality glasses, that moves along with an amputee's stump using a motion sensor. To date, six patients have been tested. Four reported a reduction in pain, and two experienced no difference.

While the work is still preliminary, Dr. Cole is optimistic about the current direction of research. "The prospects for relief from pain are probably brighter than at any time since Weir Mitchell first coined the term phantom limb pain," he says. "It's encouraging."

MIND TINGLER

MUSICAL EARWORMS

Catchy tune playing nonstop in your head? You've probably caught a musical bug called an "earworm." Simple pieces, such as advertising jingles and television theme songs, infect us most. Not a coincidence, says Oliver Sacks, neurologist and author of *Musicophilia: Tales of Music and the Brain.* The music's specially designed to "hook" listeners and "bore its way, like an earwig, into the ear or mind . . . ," he says.

Some earworms contain lyrics; others purely melodies, such as Beethoven's Fifth (ba-ba-ba-BUM). Most consist of musical fragments that can replay for hours or days before finally fading. Scientists aren't sure why songs get stuck in our heads. It could be that infectious tunes excite our brains with unusual sounds or rhythms. Earworms also may spark—and be sparked by—emotional associations, says Sacks.

Another less common way our musical senses can go awry is through musical hallucinations. One woman who Sacks describes hears everything from "Amazing Grace" to "Old Macdonald Had a Farm." At first she thought the music was playing outside somewhere, but she eventually realized her brain was creating it. In a similar case, a man said he had an "iPod in his head" that played popular songs from his childhood.

About 80 to 90 percent of people who experience musical hallucinations are older and nearly deaf, explains

Sacks. In these cases, the auditory parts of the brain appear to create the hallucinations to stay active. Not all patients follow this pattern, however. One rare twelve-year-old named Michael has been musically hallucinating since he was about five.

Catchy tunes sometimes replay in our heads, over and over and over again!

BRAINPORT:
A TASTE OF TOMORROW

heryl Schiltz still can't quite believe what happened. On a crisp November morning in 1997, she climbed out of bed and almost immediately fell to the floor. "I couldn't stand," she says. "Everything in my visual field was jumping and moving all over. It was like I had no sense of gravity . . . no sense of where I was in space. I couldn't tell what was up, down, or sideways."

Cheryl muddled through the day, crawling on floors and hugging the walls to keep upright. Two weeks later, doctors delivered the grim diagnosis: an antibiotic she'd taken for an infection had damaged her vestibular system — the organs of the inner ear that help people maintain a sense of balance. It also left her with oscillating vision, where objects sometimes appear to bounce up and down "like a bad video." Most disturbing of all, the conditions were permanent.

Stunned, but resigned to the situation, Cheryl adjusted as best she could. "The brain's very plastic," she says. "I can't say that I ever got used to it, but I was able to adapt and compensate." One way Cheryl oriented herself was through touch. "At the onset, I always had someone on my arm — someone to hang on to," she says. "When I took a shower, I'd sit in a chair."

Cheryl eventually bought a cane so she could venture outdoors. "Still, I had to stay away from uneven surfaces, low-light or no-light conditions or else I would fall to the ground," she says. "You need to have vision to tell where you are in space."

Unfortunately, Cheryl's best efforts weren't enough on the job. Returning to her sales position proved extremely difficult. "This really messes with you cognitively," she says. "Your brain is so focused on trying to stay in one place and not fall down that you have trouble with things like memory and comprehension. I always had to think about how to get from Point A to Point B." After a year and a half, Cheryl reluctantly left the work world. Without a sense of balance, her life was thrown off course. "Emotionally, physically, and psychologically, this thing was wiping me out," she says.

But Cheryl's an optimist and a fighter. While temporarily discouraged, she wasn't about to give up hope. Months later, when her doctor told her about a study aimed at helping people restore their balance, she immediately volunteered — even if it sounded a little strange.

"Dr. Paul Bach-y-Rita called me and explained the research he was doing with a device called the Tongue Display Unit [TDU]," says Cheryl. Dr. Bach-y-Rita — a neuroscientist and professor of orthopedics and rehabilitation at the University of Wisconsin, Madison — has been developing devices to substitute for senses for more than forty years. "He said that if I put this thing on my tongue, it would help me get my balance back, and I thought 'What the heck . . . what do I have to lose?'"

That "thing" Cheryl placed in the middle of her tongue was a strip of plastic containing a postage-stamp array of 144 electrodes, each of which delivered electrical impulses to her tongue.

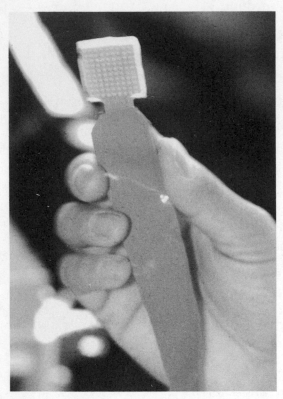

BrainPort is a sensory substitution device that uses the tongue to transmit balance and other information from the senses directly to the brain. Sensory information is delivered to the tongue via a strip of plastic containing a postage-stamp array of electrodes, as pictured above.

© AP Wide World Photos

These impulses carried sensory information about the movements of her head — all captured by a sensor mounted on top of a helmet she wore during the trials.

When activated, the TDU "buzzed" Cheryl's tongue and felt like "champagne bubbles or Pop Rocks candy," she says. The helmet sensor, called an accelerometer, sent spatial or "where-you-are-in-space" messages to the tongue. "If I drifted left or right, backwards or forwards, the accelerometer captured the sensations," she explains. "All I had to do was keep the sensation — or buzz — in the center of my tongue to ensure I was in balance."

Initially, the study involved 100-second trials. "Sometimes we'd have our eyes opened, sometimes closed, while we sat at the edge of our chairs. And lo and behold, everytime we did the trial, I was able to stay very steady. It's like all of a sudden a quietness came over me. When I didn't have [the device] on, I'd wobble." As the trials progressed, Cheryl and the researchers made a surprising — and major — discovery. "Somebody asked what would happen if I kept the device in my mouth for twenty minutes. And I said, 'I'm game. Let's try it.' So we did, and that was the first time we learned about the residual [effect]."

"I remember taking the device out of my mouth and having this feeling that something was different. It was an internal feeling. . . . For the first time in three years, I felt a release — like I was completely normal. I was sobbing and running around like crazy — they couldn't keep me still."

Cheryl's "normal" feelings only lasted about an hour, but the incident kicked off a series of trials aimed at exploring the retention effects of the balance device — now known as BrainPort. "We started doing the trials for twenty minutes, twice a day, and the residual effect became longer and stronger," she says. "My vision was clearer, even brighter. I was quick to move, and could drive again. . . . my confidence just exploded."

Today Cheryl uses a new,

Subject using the Brainport balance device.

© Andy Manis Photo

portable version of BrainPort — which features a built-in sensor and no longer requires a helmet — twice a week for twenty minutes. The tool's not a cure, but it allows her to compensate for the balance disorder so well that she's now a full-time university student majoring in rehabilitation psychology. Ultimately, she'd like to counsel other people who've acquired disabilities later in life. "Despite all the hardships, I wouldn't change a thing," says Cheryl. "I've developed a wonderful life. I wouldn't be who I am today if this didn't happen."

TONGUE TECHNOLOGY

Using the tongue to transmit sensory information may sound unusual, but it's actually the ideal organ for the job, says Yuri Danilov, neuroscientist and director of clinical research at Wicab, Inc., a company founded by Dr. Bach-y-Rita to develop BrainPort technologies. The tongue is not only a "hidden environment" that's cosmetically acceptable to patients, it's also chemically stable for conducting electrical signals. "The acidity of the saliva [pH] is constant, the temperature is constant, the humidity is constant, and it offers a flat surface with a high density of tactile nerve fibers," explains Danilov. (Tactile nerve fibers are touch receptors through which messages are communicated.) Most importantly, "the skin on our tongue sends input directly to the brain, unlike skin on most other areas of the body which go through the spinal cord." Using BrainPort, less sensory information travels from the tongue to the brain stem — the command center of the brain — through at least two nerves: the lingual nerve, which carries touch messages, and the chorda tympani nerve, which carries taste input.

Exactly how the information's processed once it leaves the brain stem remains a mystery. One theory holds that the brain has a built-in backup system for processing sensory messages. When normal pathways are blocked, it may revert to these preexisting, alternative routes, explains Danilov. With practice, the brain learns to interpret messages from the sensory substitute — in this case, tactile messages on the tongue — just as it would from the natural senses, he says.

Such versatility allows BrainPort to transmit balance information and much more, including images captured by a camera. At the University of Montreal's School of Optometry, Dr. Maurice Ptito is exploring the technology's ability to help the visually impaired. "If you train a blind person for a week with the device . . . the brain starts to analyze images from the tongue as a visual," says Danilov. "BrainPort is like a universal interface to the brain. You can use any signal from any sensor. If you can represent or record a sensation on a tactile image, the brain can interpret it."

Imagine the possibilities. BrainPort technology not only helps people compensate for sensory loss, it can enhance and extend the normal working senses — in effect, mimicking many animal "super senses." What if people could see as sharply as an eagle, hear as precisely as an owl, and track scents as discriminately as a bloodhound? Military researchers and video-game developers, among others, envision a world rich with such sensory experiences and are eagerly exploring the potential uses of BrainPort.

At the Florida Institute for Human and Machine Cognition in

Pensacola, scientists are studying how BrainPort technology can improve navigation for divers at night and in murky waters. By directing compass and sonar signals through the tongue to the brain, researchers aim to help divers detect underwater obstacles while keeping their eyes and hands free to find and identify objects as they carry out their work. The system also could bolster underwater crime-scene investigations.

Dr. Anil Raj, a research scientist at the Institute, first began working with BrainPort while looking for technology to complement

Dr. Anil Raj demonstrates the use of BrainPort as a "tongue" sonar to guide him in a pool. The technology has many uses—from sensory substitution to enhancing normal working senses.

© AP Wide World Photos

the U.S. Navy/NASA in-flight spatial orientation program for pilots called the Tactile Situational Awareness System (TSAS). Wearing a special TSAS vest, pilots can "feel" when their plane pitches and rolls — even slightly — and adjust accordingly. If the plane rolls left, for instance, pilots will feel the left side of the vest vibrate.

"In an aircraft, you can get into very, very slow roll rates, which are almost impossible to perceive," explains Dr. Raj. "A little turbulence may cause an aircraft to roll just a slight amount, but by the time you perceive it, it's already built up a great deal. . . . You may think, I've been flying at a straight level and didn't command the aircraft to roll, so it shouldn't be in a roll — maybe my instruments are wrong." You may even try to roll out of it by relying solely on your senses and end up in a deadly "graveyard" spiral, he says. "Unfortunately, this is common when people get outside of their capability."

While TSAS is a great tool, says Dr. Raj, it's "a torso-based tactile interface, and the nerve density on this part of the body is pretty sparse. This limits its ability to provide high-resolution information, for which it will never be as good as the tongue. With BrainPort, you can get a lot of robust data that can corroborate what's on your instruments," he says. "We want to provide an alternative sensing capability that allows pilots to feel changes through their tongue or body while they're doing other things, such as watching for traffic ahead or adjusting their radios. This will allow them to notice trends and understand what the aircraft's doing at all times."

As BrainPort's technology continues to evolve as a sensory orientation device, researchers are looking to develop a system that's wireless, says Dr. Raj. "That would open up many opportunities."

It also may transform the face of video games. "We've received a lot of inquiries about BrainPort from computer game companies," notes Dr. Raj, who's tested a few games and says the tool gives users a feeling of X-ray vision.

The potential applications are endless, says Danilov. The technology's still in its infancy. "You can put a signal from a compass on the tongue, and the brain will analyze the direction of movement. Or you can attach an infrared camera, ultrasound device, or chemical pollution sensor — whatever fantasy you have to sensor. Theoretically, we can use it anywhere in industry. The brain's analytical powers are unlimited — we're accessing that power to analyze information from the outside world."

FUTURE VISION

Electronic noses sniffing out disease.

Soundscapes stimulating sight.

Tongue transmitters helping orient the body.

Technology's changing the way we make sense of our world — and subsequently, the way we interact with it. "We are approaching the point where we can extend the self, virtually placing people into actual remote environments," say officials at NASA. Active volcanoes, the ocean floor, and the surface of Mars are all within reach, they report. "Robotic vehicles with the ability to convey visual and tactile information will allow us to step into these far-off and dangerous places, opening up new worlds of experience and knowledge."

As we leap forward, what new information will we discover about the abilities of our brains and the mysteries of our senses? In what novel ways will scientists bend, stretch, and imitate our sensory experiences? How will these changes influence our personal and shared perceptions of reality?

High-tech imaging machines confirm what we've suspected all along: the brain continually adapts itself to new experiences and works to compensate for losses suffered through injury. Like good neighbors, our billions of nerve cells regularly talk to each other. And, if we're lucky, the conversations grow richer with each exchange.

By enhancing our repertoire of sights, sounds, smells, tastes, and touches, we're expanding our collective worlds — both inside and out. Yet each of our individual experiences will continue to be one-of-a-kind, blending our sensory present with the past, and ensuring we carve our own unique signatures into the future.

© JUPITERIMAGES

MORE TO EXPLORE

PRINT PUBLICATIONS

Ackerman, Diane. *A Natural History of the Senses.* New York: Random House, Inc., 1990.

Cobb, Vicki. *How to Really Fool Yourself: Illusions for All Your Senses.* New York: John Wiley & Sons, Inc., 1981.

Devaney, Sherri, ed. *Extreme Super Senses (Planet's Most Extreme).* Detroit: Blackbirch Press, 2005.

Gladwell, Malcolm. *Blink: The Power of Thinking Without Thinking.* New York: Little, Brown and Company, 2005.

Herbst, Judith. *ESP (The Unexplained).* Minneapolis: Learner Publications Company, 2004.

Mass, Wendy. *A Mango-Shaped Space.* New York: Little, Brown and Company, 2003.

Newquist, HP. *The Great Brain Book: An Inside Look at the Inside of Your Head.* New York: Scholastic, 2004.

Pringle, Laurence. *Touch (Explore Your Senses).* New York: Benchmark Books, 1999.

Ruchlis, Hy. *How Do You Know It's True? Discovering the Difference Between Science and Superstition.* Amherst, New York: Prometheus Books, 1991.

Shuker, Karl P. N. *The Hidden Powers of Animals: Uncovering the Secrets of Nature.* London: Marshall Edition Ltd. (A Reader's Digest Book), 2001.

Silverstein, Alvin, Virginia Silverstein, and Laura Silverstein Nunn. *Seeing (Senses and Sensors.* Brookfield, Connecticut: Twenty-First Century Books, 2001.

Swanson, Diane. *Nibbling on Einstein's Brain: The Good, the Bad and the Bogus in Science.* Toronto: Annick Press, 2001.

Trueit, Trudi Strain. *Dreams and Sleep (Life Balance).* New York: Franklin Watts, 2004.

WEB SITES

Armagan, Esref. Esref Armagan's Web site. http://www.esrefarmagan.com

Camp Inquiry. http://campinquiry.org

Day, Sean A. Synesthesia. http://home.comcast.net/~sean.day/index.html

Exploratorium: The museum of science, art and human perception. http://www.exploratorium.edu

Howard Hughes Medical Institute. "Seeing, Hearing, and Smelling the World." http://www.hhmi.org/senses

International Association for the Study of Dreams. http://www.asdreams.org

Chudler, Eric, Ellen Kuwana, Melissa Phillips, and Marge Murray. "Neuroscience for Kids." http://faculty.washington.edu/chudler/neurok.html

Meijer, Peter B. L. "Vision Technology for the Totally Blind."
http://www.seeingwithsound.com

Nature. "Can Animals Predict Disaster?" http://www.pbs.org/wnet/nature/
animalspredict

Nova. Secrets of the Mind. http://www.pbs.org/wgbh/nova/mind

Nozek, Brian, Mahzarin Banaji, and Tony Greenwald. "Project Implicit. Implicit Association Test." http://implicit.harvard.edu/implicit/

OutOfService. "The Do-Re-Mi's of Personality: What Your Music Tastes Say About You." http://www.outofservice.com/music-personality-test

COMMON 'SENSE' TERMS

Amygdala: an almond-shaped structure in the brain that is part of the limbic system and plays a key role in memory and emotional learning

Anosmia: the inability to smell

Association cortex: areas of the cerebral cortex involved in higher mental and emotional processing of information, such as thinking and memory

Auditory system: the sensory cells in the ear and their central connections in the brain that are involved in the sense of hearing

Autokinetic effect: an illusion where a motionless point of light, such as a lone star in the sky, appears to bounce around

Brain plasticity: the brain's ability to adapt and change based on new experiences or to compensate for losses suffered through injury

BrainPort: a sensory substitution device that uses the tongue to transmit balance information and more from the senses directly to the brain

Brainstem: the major communications route by which the forebrain sends information to, and receives information from, the spinal cord and peripheral nerves. The brainstem controls our heart rate and breathing.

Clairvoyance: sensing remote events, such as a distant friend's illness

Coincidence: two or more unusual events, related by chance, and occurring at about the same time

Dreams: a sequence of images, emotions, and thoughts passing through a sleeping person's mind

Earworm: a catchy tune that sticks in our heads for hours or days before fading

EEG: Electroencephalography, the recording of brain waves by means of electrodes attached to the skull

Extrasensory perception (ESP): a general term describing ways of knowing and acquiring information—from the past, present, and/or future—said to occur apart from our normally recognized senses

Equilibrium: a state of balance

fMRI (functional Magnetic Resonance Imaging machine): a machine that uses magnetic fields and radio waves to measure blood flow in the brain and indicates the regions that are functioning during mental activity

Forebrain: the largest part of the brain, which controls intellectual functions such as thinking and speaking

Goose bumps: pebbly swellings on the skin caused by tiny muscles at the base of our body hairs that contract and lift each hair when we're cold or scared

Infrared: light invisible to humans that lies below red in the color spectrum

Infrasound: sound with a frequency that is below the range of human hearing

Intuition: knowing or sensing something instinctively, without the conscious use of rational thought processes

Limbic system: the brain's emotional control center, which includes the amygdala

Medium: a person who says he/she can communicate with the dead

Melanoma: a severe form of skin cancer that can be fatal if allowed to spread

Ménière's Disease: a disorder of the inner ear that can cause severe dizziness

Musical hallucinations: hearing music internally as if it's being played externally. It's thought that in some cases, the brain creates the hallucinations to stay active.

Neurons: nerve cells

Neuroscience: the study of the nervous system, which includes the brain, the spinal cord, and networks of sensory nerve cells, or neurons, throughout the body. Humans contain roughly 100 billion neurons, the functional units of the nervous system.

Neurotransmitter: a chemical that relays messages from one nerve cell to another

Nightmare: a deeply distressing or terrifying dream

Paranormal: experiences beyond the norm that defy explanation by science

Parapsychology: the study of paranormal phenomena

Perception: the awareness and interpretation of our environment based on information received through our senses

Perspective: an advanced technique artists use to create the illusion of a three-dimensional image on a flat surface

Phantom limb: vivid sensations of a missing part of the body, such as an arm or a leg

Pop-out visual perception test: a test with embedded figures used to identify people with synesthesia who see numbers in colors

Precognition: knowing information about events before they occur, such as accidents and natural disasters

Precognitive dream: a dream that seems to foretell a future event

Proprioception: the awareness of our body parts and their movement in space relative to each other

Prodromal dream: a dream that signals illness before a person experiences symptoms

Psychokinesis (PK): using the mind to move or change objects without touching them

Psychometry: gaining impressions—past, present, and future—of people or objects by touching or holding them

REM (rapid eye movement) sleep: a stage of sleep during which our most vivid dreams occur

Senses: the body's means of perceiving and experiencing the world. The five classic senses are seeing, hearing, smelling, tasting, and touching, but scientists have identified many more.

Sensory integration: the brain's way of organizing information it receives from our senses so we can use it effectively

Sensory Integration Dysfunction (SID): a neurological condition characterized by the brain's ineffective processing (or organizing) of information it receives from the senses

Sensory substitution: the replacement of sensory information, such as vision or balance, through another sense

Somatosensory areas: areas of the brain involved in sensations, such as pain, pressure, temperature, joint position, muscle sense, and movement

Soundscapes: highly complex sound patterns created from visual images by a technology called The vOICe. These patterns are decoded by the brain, which allows people to "see" with sound.

"Spirit" photographs: images that featured ghostly figures, often near loved ones. While many believed the photos were real, they actually were the products of trick photography.

Synapse: the place where two nerve cells communicate chemically

Synesthesia: a sensory condition characterized by the coupling of two or more senses

Synesthetes: people who have synesthesia

Tactile: pertaining to the sense of touch

Tactile Situational Awareness System (TSAS): an in-flight spatial orientation program for pilots that allows them to literally "feel" when their plane pitches and rolls

Telepathy: communicating thoughts and messages mind to mind

Thalamus: an area of the brain that processes information from the senses and relays the messages to the cerebral cortex

Transduction: the conversion of environmental stimuli, such as light, heat, or vibration, into electrical signals that can be recognized by the nervous system

Tongue Display Unit: original name of the BrainPort device

Touch: the sense by which we determine the size, shape, and texture of objects, using receptors in the skin

Vestibular labyrinth: a system of organs in the inner ear that helps people maintain a sense of balance

The vOICe: a technology that helps blind people "see" with their ears by transforming visual images into soundscapes (highly complex sound patterns) that the brain decodes back into images

SOURCE NOTES

SENSING THE WORLD

Interviews with Ian Waterman; Jonathan Cole, D.M., F.R.C.P., a consultant in clinical neurophysiology, Poole Hospital, and at Salisbury Hospital (with its spinal center), a professor at Bournemouth University, and a visiting senior lecturer, Southampton University, in the United Kingdom; and Dr. A. James Hudspeth, researcher for the Howard Hughes Medical Institute and head of the Laboratory of Sensory Neuroscience at the Rockefeller University in New York.

Ackerman, Diane. *A Natural History of the Senses.* New York: Vintage Books, 1991.

Colavita, Francis B. "Sensation, Perception, and the Aging Process," the Great Courses, Lecture Transcript and Course Guidebook, the Teaching Company, Chantilly, Virginia. http://www.TEACH12.com.

Cole, Jonathan. *Pride and a Daily Marathon.* Cambridge: The MIT Press, 1995, p. 12.

Durie, Bruce. "Senses special: Doors of perception," *New Scientist,* no. 2484 (January 29, 2005).

Howard Hughes Medical Institute. "Seeing, Hearing, and Smelling the World." Chevy Chase, MD,1995. http://www.hhmi.org/senses

Hudspeth, A. James, and Jeremy H. Nathans, "Senses and Sensitivity: Neuronal Alliances for Sight and Sound." Howard Hughes Medical Institute Holiday Lectures on Science, Chevy Chase, MD, December 1997.

Ramachandran, Vilayanur S. *A Brief Tour of Human Consciou5ness.* New York: Pi Press, 2004.

Sacks, Oliver. *The Man Who Mistook His Wife for a Hat.* New York: Summit Books, 1985.

Smith, Jillyn. *Senses and Sensibilities.* New York: John Wiley & Sons, 1989.

MIND TINGLER: ATTENTION-GETTERS

Interview with Dr. A. James Hudspeth, researcher for the Howard Hughes Medical Institute and head of the Laboratory of Sensory Neuroscience at The Rockefeller University in New York.

Howard Hughes Medical Institute. "Seeing, Hearing, and Smelling the World." Chevy Chase, MD, 1995. http://www.hhmi.org/senses

THE SIXTH SENSE

Interviews with Annette Martin, psychic detective, Closure4U; Tom Gilovich, professor and chairperson, department of psychology, Cornell University; John Palmer, director of research, Rhine Research Center; and Ronald Rensink, Ph.D., associate professor of computer science and psychology at the University of British Columbia.

Dimitrius, Jo-Ellan. *Reading People: How to Understand People and Predict Their Behavior—Anytime, Anyplace.* New York: Ballantine Books, 1998.

Gilovich, Thomas. *How We Know What Isn't So: The Fallibility of Human Reason in Everyday Life.* New York: The Free Press, 1991.

Meade, W. W. "Secret of the Lost Stone," *Reader's Digest,* November 1999.

Myers, David G. "Is There ESP? Putting ESP to the Experimental Test." http://davidmyers.org/Brix?pageID=61&article_part=4

Reaney, Patricia. "The fear of 'haunted' houses explained," Reuters, Sept. 8, 2003.

Wiseman, Richard. *Deception & Self-Deception: Investigating Psychics.* Amherst, New York: Prometheus Books, 1997.

Wiseman, Richard, and Emma Greening. "The Mind Machine: A Mass Participation Experiment into the Possible Existence of Extrasensory Perception," *British Journal of Psychology* 93, (November 2002): 487–499.

ANIMAL SUPER SENSES

Interviews with Michelle Heupel, Ph.D., staff scientist and program manager at the Mote Marine Laboratory in Sarasota, FL; Caitlin O'Connell-Rodwell, Ph.D., research associate at Stanford University; Bill Barklow, Ph.D., biologist at Framingham State College; John Caprio, Ph.D., biologist at Louisiana State University; Nicholas Broffman, executive director of the Pine Street Foundation, San Anselmo, CA; and Debbie Marvit-McGlothin.

Bat Echolocation, Maryland Department of Natural Resources, October 2004.

Ikeya, Motoji. *Earthquakes and Animals: From Folk Legends to Science.* Singapore: World Scientific Publishing Company, 2004.

————"Earthquakes and Animals—From Folk Legends to Science: Electromagnetic Seismology through Automatic Observation Networks," research paper presented at the International Conference in Commemoration of the 5th Anniversary of the 1999 Chi-Chi Earthquake, Taiwan, September 2004.

Ivanyi, Craig. "Rattlesnakes," Arizona-Sonora Desert Museum, 2000. http://www.desertmuseum.org/books/nhsd_rattlesnakes.php.

Kenneally, Christine. "Surviving the Tsunami: What Sri Lanka's Animals Knew That Humans Didn't," *Slate,* December 30, 2004. http://www.slate.com/id/2111608/.

Lindsay, Bethany. "The Compasses of Birds," *The Science Creative Quarterly,* June 6, 2005. http://www.scq.ubc.ca/the-compasses-of-birds/.

McCulloch, Michael, et al. "Diagnostic Accuracy of Canine Scent Detection in Early- and Late-Stage Lung and Breast Cancers," *Integrative Cancer Therapies* 5, no. 1 (2006).

Oldenburg, Don. "A Sense of Doom: Animal Instinct For Disaster: Scientists Investigate Wildlife's Possible Warning Systems," *Washington Post,* Jan. 8, 2005. http://www.washingtonpost.com/wp-dyn/articles/A57653-2005Jan7.html.

Orey, Cal. *The Man Who Predicts Earthquakes: Jim Berkland, Maverick Geologist.* Boulder, Colorado: Sentient Publications, 2006.

Sabine, Charles. "Senses helped animals survive the tsunami," MSNBC, Jan. 6, 2005. http://www.msnbc.msn.com/id/6795562/.

McNeil, Donald G., Jr. "Dogs Excel on Smell Test to Find Cancer," *New York Times*, January 17, 2006. http://www.nytimes.com/2006/01/17/health/17dog.html.

Wikramanayake, Eric. "Using GIS to Assess Elephants' Response to Tsunami: No Behavioral Response of Elephants to Tsunami," Smithsonian National Zoological Park. http://nationalzoo.si.edu/ConservationAndScience/ConservationGIS/projects/asian_elephants/tsunami.cfm.

MIND TINGLER: SENSE-SATIONS

"Sense of Smell," *The Infinite Mind*, radio broadcast hosted by Dr. Fred Goodwin and produced by Lichtenstein Creative Media, Cambridge, MA, April 30, 2003.

Cobb, Vicki. *How to R elf: Illusions for All Your Senses*. New York: John Wiley & Sons, 1981.

INTUITION: MORE THAN A FEELING

Interview with Sam Gosling, Ph.D., personality/social psychologist at the University of Texas at Austin.

"Don't Race to Judgment, What to Say When," *US News and World Report*, December 18, 2005. http://health.usnews.com/usnews/health/articles/051226/26spirit.race.htm

Gladwell, Malcolm. *Blink: The Power of Thinking Without Thinking*. New York: Little, Brown and Company, 2005.

Gosling, Samuel D., et al. "A Room with a Cue: Judgments of Personality Based on Offices and Bedrooms," *Journal of Personality and Social Psychology* 82 (2002), 379–398.

Greer, Mark. "When Intuition Misfires," *Monitor on Psychology*, March 2005. www.apa.org/monitor/mar05/misfires.html.

Klein, Gary. *Sources of Power: How People Make Decisions*. Cambridge: MIT Press Reprint, 1999.

Myers, David G. *Intuition: Its Powers and Perils*. London: Yale University Press, 2002.

————— "The Powers and Perils of Intuition," (essay, first draft), Dec. 21, 2006.

Winerman, Lea. "What We Know Without Knowing How," American Psychological Association's *Monitor on Psychology* 36, no. 3 (March 2005). http://www.apa.org/monitor/mar05/knowing.html

Rentfrow, Peter J., and Samuel D. Gosling. "Message in a Ballad: The Role of Music Preferences in Interpersonal Perception," *Psychological Science* 17, no. 3 (2006): 236–242.

————— "The Do Re Mi's of Everyday Life: The Structure and Personality Correlates of Music Preferences," *Journal of Personality and Social Psychology* 84, no. 6 (2003): 1236–1256.

————— Frequently Asked Questions—The Do-Re-Mi's of Personality: What Your Music Tastes Say About You. http://www.outofservice.com/music-personality-test/faq/.

Project Implicit. http://projectimplicit.net/generalinfo.php.

Coincidences: Twists of Fate or Flukes?

Interviews with Karl Sigman, Ph.D., professor in the department of operations research at Columbia University in New York; Hollis Long; and Josh Tenenbaum, assistant professor of computational cognitive science at the Massachusetts Institute of Technology.

Anderson, Joan Wester. "Someone to Watch Over You: True Stories of Guardian Angels," *BottomLine*, December 1, 2005.

Hopcke, Robert H. *There Are No Accidents: Synchronicity and the Stories of Our Lives*. New York: Riverhead Books, 1997.

Gibb, Sarah. "Science Probes Mystery of Mind Over Matter: Sept. 11 Lotto Coincidence Could Be Latest Example of Power of Unknown Effect," *Saskatoon StarPhoenix*, September 14, 2002.

Griffiths, Tom L., and Joshua B. Tenenbaum. "From mere Coincidences to Meaningful Discoveries," *Cognition* 103, no. 2 (2007): 180–226.

———. "Statistics and the Bayesian Mind," *Significance*, September 2006.

McBride, Jessica. "A Sudden Breeze, and Loved Ones Seem Near," *Milwaukee Journal Sentinel*, Sept. 12, 2002.

Neimark, Jill. "Pattern and Circumstance: The Power of Coincidence," *Psychology Today*, July/August 2004.

Rushnell, SQuire. *When God Winks: How the Power of Coincidence Guides Your Life*. New York: Atria Books, 2001.

DREAM WORLDS

Interviews with Rita Dwyer and Robert Van de Castle, Ph.D., past presidents of the International Association for the Study of Dreams; Rosalind Cartwright, Ph.D., chairman of the department of psychology and founder of the Sleep Disorder Service and Research Center at Rush University Medical Center in Chicago.

Duda, Jeremy. "Study Shows Test Cramming Has Negative Effects on Grades," *Arizona Daily Wildcat*, Feb. 2, 2001.

Halber, Deborah. "Memory Experts Show Sleeping Rats May Have Visual Dreams," MIT News Office, Dec. 18, 2006.

Kantrowitz, Barbara, and Karen Springen. "What Dreams Are Made of," *Newsweek*, August 2006.

Linn, Virginia. "Dreams: From Falling to Failing, It's the Same Old Story," *Pittsburgh Post–Gazette*, December 7, 2003.

Nye, Risa. "Prodromal Dreaming: Listening to Subconscious Medical Diagnosis," *San Francisco Chronicle*, Nov. 13, 2005.

Spice, Byron. "The Science of Dreams," *Pittsburgh Post–Gazette*, Dec. 7, 2003.

Barrett, Deirdre. *The Committee of Sleep: How Artists, Scientists, and Athletes Use Dreams for Creative Problem Solving—and How You Can Too.* New York: Crown Publishers, 2001.

Van de Castle, Robert L. *Our Dreaming Mind.* New York: Ballantine Books, 1994.

"Scientists Learn to Program Human Dreams: Research Adds to Links Between Dreams and Learning, Creativity," Harvard Medical School Office of Public Affairs, October 12, 2000.

Domhoff, William. Interview by Todd Mundt, *The Todd Mundt Show*, WUOM, Ann Arbor, Michigan, June 3. 2002.

MIND TINGLER: DREAM CATCHING

Interviews with Rosalind Cartwright, Ph.D., chairman of the department of psychology and founder of the Sleep Disorder Service and Research Center at Rush University Medical Center in Chicago; and Rita Dwyer, past president of the International Association for the Study of Dreams.

PURPLE NUMBERS AND POINTY CHICKENS

Interviews with Carol Crane, Ph.D.; Sean Day, Ph.D.; Dr. Richard Cytowic; and Edward M. Hubbard, Ph.D. Information also provided by Julia Simner, Ph.D., synesthesia researcher at the University of Edinburgh in the United Kingdom.

Cytowic, Richard E. *The Man Who Tasted Shapes*, Cambridge: MIT Press, 1998.

———— "Touching Tastes, Seeing Smells—and Shaking Up Brain Science," *Cerebrum* 4, no. 3 (Summer 2002): 7–26.

Ramachandran, Vilayanur S. *A Brief Tour of Human Consciou5ness.* New York: Pi Press, 2004.

Ramachandran, Vilayanur S., and Edward M. Hubbard. "Hearing Colors, Tasting Shapes," *Scientific American Mind* 288, no. 5 (May 2003).

———— "Synaesthesia: A Window into Perception, Thought and Language," *Journal of Consciousness Studies* 18, no. 12 (2001): 3–34.

Simner, Julia, et al. "Synaesthesia: The prevalence of atypical cross-modal experiences," *Perception* 35 (August 2006): 1024–1033.

MIND TINGLER: SYNESTHESIA Q&A

Adapted from the synesthesia FAQ developed by Julia Simner, Ph.D., at the University of Edinburgh in the United Kingdom (syn6th.com/english/faq.htm), with multi-language answer provided by Edward Hubbard, Ph.D.

ARTISTIC TOUCH

Interviews with Joan Eroncel; John M. Kennedy, professor of psychology, chair, Department of Life Sciences, University of Toronto at Scarborough; and Dr. Alvaro Pascual-Leone, professor of neurology at Harvard Medical School and director of the Center for Noninvasive Brain Stimulation at Beth Israel Deaconess Hospital.

Armagan, Esref. Esref Armagan's Web site. http://www.esrefarmagan.com

Motluk, Alison. "The Art of Seeing Without Sight," *New Scientist*, January 29, 2005.

Feinberg, Cara. "Old Brain, New Tricks," *The Boston Globe*, January 15, 2006.

THE SOUND OF SIGHT

Interviews with Pat Fletcher and Dr. Peter Meier, inventor of The vOICe.

Meijer, Peter. "Seeing with Sound" Web site. http://www.seeingwithsound.com.

Motluk, Alison. "Seeing With Your Ears," *New York Times*, December 11, 2005.

Motluk, Alison. "The Science of Seeing with Sound," documentary by

Alison Motluk on *Quirks & Quarks*, Canadian CBC Radio One hosted by Bob McDonald, April 2, 2005.

MIND TINGLER: SENSES OUT OF SYNC

Ayres, A. Jean. *Sensory Integration and the Child*. Los Angeles: Western Psychological Services, 1987.

BRAIN PHANTOMS: HAUNTING THE BODY

Interviews with Tom Whittaker (http://www.tomwhittaker.com); and Jonathan Cole, D.M., F.R.C.P., a consultant in clinical neurophysiology, Poole Hospital, and at Salisbury Hospital (with its spinal center), a professor at Bournemouth University, and a visiting senior lecturer, Southampton University, in the United Kingdom.

Discover magazine, "Phantom Limb—Research Indicates People Born Without a Limb Experience Phenomenon of Phantom Limbs," February 1998.

Nova. "Secrets of the Mind," WGBH Educational Foundation, Boston, Massachusetts, PBS, October 2001.

Cole, Jonathan. "Phantom Limb Pain," The Wellcome Trust Web site. http://www.wellcome.ac.uk/en/pain/microsite/medicine2.html

Mitchell, S. Weir. *Injuries of Nerves and Their Consequences*. New York: J.B. Lippincott, 1872.

Ramachandran, Vilayanur S. *A Brief Tour of Human Consciou5ness*. New York: Pi Press, 2004.

Sherman, Richard A. "Pain After Amputation: A Lifelong Problem?" Behavioral Medicine Research and Training Foundation, October 1997. http://www.behavmedfoundation.org/pdf/painamputation1.pdf

The Wellcome Trust Web site, "Virtual Pain Relief: Giving Amputees a 'Virtual Limb' Could Provide Relief from Phantom Limb Pain," http://www.wellcome.ac.uk/doc_WTD004723.html

Whittaker, Tom, with Johnny Dodd. *Higher Purpose: The Heroic Story of the First Disabled Man to Conquer Everest.* Washington DC: Lifeline Press, 2001.

———— *Phantoms in the Brain.* New York: HarperCollins, 1999.

Phantom Limb segment, Show #204, "Where Am I?" Radio Lab, WNYC New York Public Radio, May 5, 2006.

MIND TINGLER: MUSICAL EARWORMS

"Book Tour: Oliver Sacks Observes the Mind Through Music," National Public Radio, podcast, Nov. 13, 2007.

Sacks, Oliver. *Musicophilia: Tales of Music and the Brain.* New York: Alfred A. Knopf, 2007.

BRAINPORT: A TASTE OF TOMORROW

Interviews with Cheryl Schiltz, BrainPort technologies client; Yuri Danilov, neuroscientist and director of clinical research at Wicab, Inc., a company founded by Dr. Paul Bach-y-Rita to develop BrainPort technologies; and Dr. Anil Raj, a research scientist at the Florida Institute for Human and Machine Cognition in Pensacola.

BrainPort Technologies Web site, http://www.wicab.us.

Blakeslee, Sandra. "New Tools to Help Patients Reclaim Damaged Senses," *New York Times,* November 23, 2004.

Manning, Joe. "Device May Be New Pathway to the Brain: Researchers Invent System That Helps with Balance, Sight," *Milwaukee Journal-Sentinel,* December 7, 2004.

Nelson, Melissa. "Warriors of the Future Will 'Taste' Battlefield," *Associated Press,* April 22, 2006.

FUTURE VISION

The National Aeronautics and Space Administration (NASA) Exploration Systems Mission Directorate Education Outreach Web site, "Extending the Senses—Technology and Our Universe Experiences." http://www.weboflife.nasa.gov/currentResearch/currentResearchGeneralArchives/senses.htm.

TERMS

Some terms adapted from the glossary of "Seeing, Hearing, and Smelling the World: New Findings Help Scientists Make Sense of Our Senses," Howard Hughes Medical Institute, Chevy Chase, MD, 1995.

INDEX